Encountering the God of Faith, Hope, and Love in the Bible

George M. Smiga
with Little Rock Scripture Study staff

Little Rock Scripture Study

LITURGICAL PRESS
Collegeville, Minnesota

littlerockscripture.org

Nihil obstat for the commentary text by George M. Smiga: Reverend Robert C. Harren, J.C.L., *Censor Librorum*.
Imprimatur for the commentary text by George M. Smiga: ✠ Most Rev. Patrick M. Neary, C.S.C., Bishop of St. Cloud, May 5, 2025

Cover design by John Vineyard. Interior art by Ned Bustard.

This symbol indicates material that was created by Little Rock Scripture Study to supplement the biblical text and commentary. Some of these inserts first appeared in the *Little Rock Catholic Study Bible*; others were created specifically for this book by George Smiga and Amy Ekeh.

Library of Congress Cataloging-in-Publication Data

Names: Smiga, George M., 1948- author. | Little Rock Scripture Study Staff, author.
Title: Encountering the God of faith, hope, and love in the Bible / George M. Smiga, with Little Rock scripture study staff.
Description: Collegeville, MN : Liturgical Press, [2025] | Series: Little Rock scripture study | Summary: "In Encountering the God of Faith, Hope, and Love in the Bible, Fr. George Smiga explores how God is revealed through various stages of salvation history-from the call of Abraham through the resurrection of Jesus-and how faith, hope, and love have evolved as our understanding of God grows. Commentary, study and reflection questions, prayers, and access to online lectures are included. 6 lessons"— Provided by publisher.
Identifiers: LCCN 2025005855 (print) | LCCN 2025005856 (ebook) | ISBN 9798400800504 (trade paperback) | ISBN 9798400800528 (epub)
Subjects: LCSH: God— Biblical teaching. | Theological virtues— Biblical teaching. | Bible— Theology— Study and teaching. | Catholic Church— Doctrines. | BISAC: RELIGION / Biblical Studies / Bible Study Guides | RELIGION / Christianity / Catholic
Classification: LCC BS544 .S63 2025 (print) | LCC BS544 (ebook) | DDC 231— dc23/eng/20250416
LC record available at https://lccn.loc.gov/2025005855
LC ebook record available at https://lccn.loc.gov/2025005856

Encountering the God of Faith, Hope, and Love in the Bible

TABLE OF CONTENTS

Wrap-Up Lectures and Discussion Tips for Facilitators are available for each lesson at no charge. Find them online at LittleRockScripture.org/Lectures/FaithHopeLove.

Welcome

The Bible is at the heart of what it means to be a Christian. It is the Spirit-inspired word of God for us. It reveals to us the God who created, redeemed, and guides us still. It speaks to us personally and as a church. It forms the basis of our public liturgical life and our private prayer lives. It urges us to live worthily and justly, to love tenderly and wholeheartedly, and to be a part of building God's kingdom here on earth.

Though it was written a long time ago, in the context of a very different culture, the Bible is no relic of the past. Catholic biblical scholarship is among the best in the world, and in our time and place, we have unprecedented access to it. By making use of solid scholarship, we can discover much about the ancient culture and religious practices that shaped those who wrote the various books of the Bible. With these insights, and by praying with the words of Scripture, we allow the words and images to shape us as disciples. By sharing our journey of faithful listening to God's word with others, we have the opportunity to be stretched in our understanding and to form communities of love and learning. Ultimately, studying and praying with God's word deepens our relationship with Christ.

Encountering the God of Faith, Hope, and Love in the Bible

The resource you hold in your hands is divided into six lessons. Each lesson involves personal prayer and study using this book and the experience of group prayer, discussion, and wrap-up lecture.

If you are using this resource in the context of a small group, we suggest that you meet six times, discussing one lesson per meeting. Allow about 90 minutes for the small group gathering. Small groups function best with eight to twelve people to ensure good group dynamics and to allow all to participate as they wish.

Some groups choose to have an initial gathering before their regular sessions begin. This allows an opportunity to meet one another, pass out books, and, if desired, view the optional intro lecture for this study available on the "Resources" page of the Little Rock Scripture Study website (littlerockscripture.org). Please note that there is only one intro lecture for two-part studies.

Every Bible study group is a little bit different. Some of our groups like to break each lesson up into two weeks of study so they are reading less each week and have more time to discuss the questions together at their weekly gatherings. If your group wishes to do this, simply agree how much of each lesson will be read each week, and only answer the questions that correspond to the material you read. Wrap-up lectures can then be viewed at the end of every other meeting rather than at the end of every meeting. Of course, this will mean that your study will last longer, and your group will meet more times.

WHAT MATERIALS WILL YOU USE?

The materials in this book include:

- Scripture passages to be studied, using the New American Bible, Revised Edition as the translation.
- Commentary by George M. Smiga.
- Occasional inserts highlighting elements of the Scripture passages being studied. Some of these appear also in the *Little Rock Catholic Study Bible* while others are supplied by the author and staff writers.
- Questions for study, reflection, and discussion at the end of each lesson.
- Opening and closing prayers for each lesson, as well as other prayer forms available in the closing pages of the book.

In addition, there are wrap-up lectures available for each lesson. Your group may choose to purchase a DVD containing these lectures or make use of the video lectures available online at no charge. The link to these free lectures is: LittleRockScripture.org/Lectures/FaithHopeLove. Of course, if your group has access to qualified speakers, you may choose to have live presentations.

Each person will need a current translation of the Bible. We recommend the *Little Rock Catholic Study Bible*, which makes use of the New American Bible, Revised Edition. Other translations, such as the New Jerusalem Bible or the New Revised Standard Version: Catholic Edition, would also work well.

HOW WILL YOU USE THESE MATERIALS?

Prepare in advance

Using Lesson One as an example:

- Begin with a simple prayer like the one found on page 11.

- Read the assigned material for Lesson One (pages 12–22) so that you are prepared for the weekly small group session.
- Answer the questions, Exploring Lesson One, found at the end of the assigned reading, pages 23–25.
- Use the Closing Prayer on page 26 when you complete your study. This prayer may be used again when you meet with the group.

Meet with your small group

- After introductions and greetings, allow time for prayer (about 5 minutes) as you begin the group session. You may use the prayer on page 11 (also used by individuals in their preparation) or use a prayer of your choosing.
- Spend about 45–50 minutes discussing the responses to the questions that were prepared in advance. You may also develop your discussion further by responding to questions and interests that arise during the discussion and faith-sharing itself.
- Close the discussion and faith-sharing with prayer, about 5–10 minutes. You may use the Closing Prayer at the end of each lesson or one of your choosing at the end of the book. It is important to allow people to pray for personal and community needs and to give thanks for how God is moving in your lives.
- View the wrap-up lecture associated with each lesson (about 15 minutes). You may watch the lecture online, use a DVD, or provide a live lecture by a qualified local speaker. View the lecture together at the end of the session or, if your group runs out of time, you may invite group members to watch the lecture on their own time after the discussion.

A note to individuals

- If you are using this resource for individual study, simply move at your own pace. Take as much time as you need to read, study, and pray with the material.
- If you would like to share this experience with others, consider inviting a friend or family member to join you for your next study. Even a small group of two or three provides an opportunity for fruitful dialog and faith-sharing!

Encountering the God of Faith, Hope, and Love in the Bible

LESSON ONE

Faith and Hope in the God of the Family

Begin your personal study and group discussion with a simple and sincere prayer such as:

Prayer

Lord God, help us listen with the ears of our hearts as we spend time with your word. Reveal yourself to us today as you have revealed yourself through the ages, and strengthen in us your gifts of faith, hope, and love.

Read pages 12–22, Lesson One.

Respond to the questions on pages 23–25, Exploring Lesson One.

The Closing Prayer on page 26 is for your personal use and may be used at the end of group discussion.

INTRODUCTION

When Christians hear of the triad "faith, hope, and love," we usually think of three habits or virtues. This is understandable because our catechetical tradition presents them as such. The *Catechism of the Catholic Church* calls faith, hope, and love "theological virtues" because they make us capable of participating in the life of God: "The theological virtues relate directly to God. They dispose Christians to live in a relationship with the Holy Trinity. They have the One and Triune God for their origin, motive, and object" (1812). Faith, hope, and love are the highest gifts because they have the highest purpose: They make our relationship with God possible.

The Bible also speaks of faith, hope, and love. It does not refer to them as virtues; nevertheless, the biblical understanding of this holy triad agrees with the *Catechism*: They are three gifts that allow the human person to know and serve God.

These three gifts are best understood together. When we first considered a Bible study on faith, hope, and love for Little Rock Scripture Study, we entertained the possibility of publishing three separate volumes, one for each gift. But as our discussion continued, it became obvious that in the Scriptures these three gifts are too intertwined to be presented separately. This volume is the result of that insight. It will present faith, hope, and love as three interconnected dimensions of the divine-human relationship. They are three essential ways we participate in the life of God.

Because faith, hope, and love enable our relationship with God, their significance is determined by how we understand God. The appreciation of who God is and what God has done deepens as we move through the Bible. Our ability to encounter God deepens as well. What it means to be in relationship with God is considerably different in the book of Genesis, for example, than in the First Letter to the Corinthians—although it will be a goal of this study to show that a profound continuity remains.

Studying faith, hope, and love in the Bible is not an abstract, philosophical effort. This holy triad offers three ways to understand a relationship—our relationship with God. Of course, this is a mammoth undertaking. Therefore, we must be satisfied simply to address the highlights and contours of its development. That is what this volume attempts to do. But before we begin, we will briefly discuss the focus of each of the three gifts and how they relate to one another.

Faith

There is no single word for "faith" in the Hebrew Scriptures (Old Testament). There is, rather, a cluster of words that carry the sense of reliability, trustworthiness, confidence, or belief. As verbs, they express being firmly set on something, having confidence in something, or holding something to be true.

When these words are directed toward God, they describe a relationship, because faith is directed to a person in whom we place our confidence. Faith, in the biblical sense, is not intellectual assent to a set of theological dogmas, like those found in a creed. It is entering into and clinging to a personal relationship with God, who is recognized as trustworthy.

Faith, hope, and love are three gifts that make our relationship with God possible.

The New Testament employs the Greek word *pistis* to describe faith. The term carries forward the sense of the Hebrew Scriptures: entering into and holding on to a personal relationship with God.

Hope

The Hebrew Scriptures also use a variety of terms for "hope," whereas the New Testament regularly employs one word (*elpis*) to describe it. What the two testaments share in common is the conviction that hope is essential to and is derived from a relationship with God.

Faith and hope are closely connected. If faith is entering into a relationship with God, hope describes what we expect from that relationship and what we believe God will give us. Hope, then, is directed less by our desires and expectations and more by God's intention and power. The more we understand who God is and what God can do, the more hope expands.

As the biblical tradition develops over time, the awareness of God's power increases and the scope of God's intention for humanity is clarified. Faith and hope follow this development. As the appreciation of God and what we can expect from God increases, there is simply more in which to believe and hope.

We will follow the biblical development of faith and hope in the first four lessons of this study. Lesson One is "Faith and Hope in the God of the Family." Here we will examine the beginnings of faith and hope in the narratives of Genesis concerning the patriarchs and matriarchs of Israel. Lesson Two is "Faith and Hope in the God of the Nations." Our focus here will be on the exodus, the covenant at Sinai, and Israel's accounts of the creation of the world. Lesson Three is "Faith and Hope in the God of the World to Come." Here we will explore the impact of Israel's exile in Babylon, the growing desire for a better world, and the emergence of belief in the resurrection of the dead. Lesson Four is "Faith and Hope in the Gospel." This lesson will examine how our understanding of God's intention and power are enlarged and fulfilled by the mission of Jesus.

As we move through these first four lessons, we will also identify ten characteristics the Bible offers us to describe our relationship with the God of faith, hope, and love. Some of these characteristics emerge in the earliest passages that describe the divine-human relationship. Others are revealed later in Israel's experience. But all ten continue as viable descriptions of our relationship with God today.

Love

The biblical concept of love is extremely wide. It can refer to affection, attraction, sexual activity, friendship, loyalty, covenant, kindness, or mercy. In the Bible, love calls forth qualities of intimate knowledge, devotion, loyalty, and responsibility. This study will focus primarily on theological love, the love that characterizes the divine-human relationship. Love is what grounds the relationship between God and us.

Lesson Five will explore God's love for us. It will show how the Bible presents God's love as inexplicable, scandalous, universal, and incarnate. Lesson Six will discuss love from the other side of the relationship: our love for God. We will discover a continuity within the Bible that links our love for God with our love for our neighbor, especially our enemies and those who are marginalized.

Contemporary Relevance

In my two other books for Little Rock Scripture Study (*Angels in the Bible* and *The Holy Spirit in the Bible*), I included sections entitled *Contemporary Relevance* that offer suggestions for how particular biblical passages might connect to our lives today. Because these sections were positively received by our participants, I have also included them in this study. As always, my suggestions in these *Contemporary Relevance* sections should not be considered complete or definitive. I offer them only to encourage further reflection on faith, hope, and love and their meaning for your life. I hope they will enrich your reading of these biblical texts and your discussions and faith-sharing with one another.

FAITH AND HOPE IN THE GOD OF THE FAMILY

The Relationship Begins with Abraham

We have described biblical faith as entering into and clinging to a personal relationship with God. Our relationship with God became possible at a specific moment in history. Where and when did it begin? Those who are familiar with the Bible might be inclined to turn to the creation stories of Genesis 1–2. After all, what is earlier than creation? But, as we will see in Lesson Two, these profound narratives of the world's beginning derive from later periods of Israel's history. The first scriptural recounting of faith in God is to be found in the narratives of Genesis 12–50. Although these stories of Abraham and Sarah, Isaac and Rebekah, Jacob and Leah and Rachel, and Joseph were heavily edited by later biblical authors, most scholars recognize that the historical traditions within them mark the beginning of our relationship with God.

Enough historical material can be gleaned from these early narratives to suggest that our relationship with God began around 1,850 years before the birth of Christ, in Mesopotamia, in the city of Haran, a busy trade center located in what is today southeast Turkey. There, a man who had migrated with his family from Ur, another city of Mesopotamia, heard the voice of God. The man's name was Abraham (see insert on p. 15). His communication with God initiated the faith tradition of Jews, Christians, and Muslims. So important was this encounter between God and Abraham that the Hebrew Bible provides three versions of it. We will examine two of them in depth, demonstrating how each narrative establishes important dimensions of our relationship with God that continue to be relevant to this day.

Abraham and the God Who Initiates, Creates Community, and Journeys with Us

Genesis 12:1-9

Abram's Call and Migration. 1The LORD said
to Abram: Go forth from your land, your rela-
tives, and from your father's house to a land that
I will show you. 2I will make of you a great nation,
and I will bless you; I will make your name great,
so that you will be a blessing. 3I will bless those
who bless you and curse those who curse you. All
the families of the earth will find blessing in you.
4Abram went as the LORD directed him, and
Lot went with him. Abram was seventy-five years
old when he left Haran. 5 Abram took his wife
Sarai, his brother's son Lot, all the possessions that
they had accumulated, and the persons they had
acquired in Haran, and they set out for the land
of Canaan. When they came to the land of Ca-
naan, 6Abram passed through the land as far as
the sacred place at Shechem, by the oak of Moreh.
The Canaanites were then in the land.
7The LORD appeared to Abram and said: To
your descendants I will give this land. So Abram
built an altar there to the LORD who had appeared
to him. 8From there he moved on to the hill coun-
try east of Bethel, pitching his tent with Bethel to
the west and Ai to the east. He built an altar there
to the LORD and invoked the LORD by name.
9Then Abram journeyed on by stages to the Negeb.

The voice of God bursts forth in Genesis 12 without context or preparation. We are not told on what day or in what circumstance Abraham hears the voice. Does it come during work or while Abraham rests? Is he alone or with others? All we know is that Abraham understands he is being addressed. The voice comes without identification—no name, no reference to the past—only a command: "Go forth." Nor is Abraham told where to go beyond to "a land that I will show you" (v. 1). It is remarkable how little explanation is provided. All that Abraham is given is a promise: the promise of land and offspring.

"Land" here should not be understood in financial terms, as a gift of real estate. It is a place where Abraham and those who are with him can permanently live, no longer wandering from one place to another. The God who speaks to Abraham is the God of the Family. Offspring and a place to flourish are necessary if family is to exist.

Land and offspring are the deepest desire of Abraham's heart. From Genesis 11:30, we know that Abraham's wife, Sarah, has been unable to conceive a child. Abraham and Sarah's hope for a family has turned to hopelessness. Yet it is into that hopelessness that the voice speaks, addressing the childless father and promising what seems impossible.

What can one do when addressed by such a voice? Even though it is possible that the voice is an illusion or deception, Abraham does what the voice directs him to do. He goes (v. 4). Leaving Haran could not have been easy. Although Abraham is a wanderer, he has made a good life in Haran. Not only is he living with his extended family, but he has accumulated wealth and a retinue of people who accompany him (vv. 4-5). Moreover, Haran—a significant crossroads of Mesopotamia—is a vibrant, cosmopolitan, and progressive city. Its culture in this period is among the most advanced in the world. Yet Abraham leaves this land, his relatives, and his father's house for an undisclosed destination because he hears the voice of God.

Why does Abraham leave the security and prosperity of Haran on the authority of an unidentified voice? Perhaps it is because the voice understands that, for all its attractions, Haran is, for Abraham, still barren. Although Haran is in a good land, it is not Abraham's land. Although Abraham is surrounded by relatives, he and Sarah do not have children of their own. So when the voice promises land and offspring, Abraham trusts in the One who speaks to him—not because the promise can be tested or verified but because the One who addresses him understands the deepest desire of his heart.

This is the earliest memory of faith in the Bible. Here Abraham becomes the model of faith for all subsequent believers. Those who enter a relationship with God do so not because their choice is always obvious or convincing but because, somehow, they sense that the One who calls them knows them better than they know themselves. In some way, despite all the good things we may already possess, there remains in each one of us a barrenness that, when addressed, can lead to faith.

Here, for the first time in our study, we are able to identify the close connection between faith and hope. Abraham leaves Haran in the hope that the promise given to him will satisfy his deepest desire. His hope is grounded in his faith in the God who speaks to him. There can be no promise without a Promise-Maker. There can be no hope without faith. It is because Abraham is willing to enter into a relationship with the God who knows his barrenness that he dares to hope in the promise of family.

In Genesis, Abraham and Sarah are also known as Abram and Sarai. Abram/Abraham means "exalted father," and Sarai/Sarah means "princess." In Genesis 17, God changes their names from Abram/Sarai to Abraham/Sarah, reflecting the frequent biblical practice of associating a **new name** with a new role (e.g., Gen 32:29; Matt 16:18). For simplicity we will use "Abraham" and "Sarah" within the text of this book.

Characteristics of God. Genesis 12:1-9 shows us three characteristics of the God who calls us into a relationship of faith and hope.

(1) A God Who Freely Initiates. Faith is entering into and clinging to a relationship with God. We cannot initiate such a relationship. God is the superior partner, infinitely beyond our power to direct or control. God, then, must make the first move. Therefore, in a real sense we cannot "find" faith or "give" faith to another. God is the One who must find and give. As important as it is for us to respond, God's invitation is primary. It is foundational to our faith tradition that God is willing to initiate a personal relationship with us, as God did with Abraham.

Moreover, our relationship with God is a grace, a free gift. Faith in God is never earned or merited. God calls Abraham without conditions. There is no arrangement that God will do this if Abraham does that. After the call to go forth, five statements outline what God will do for Abraham: "I will make of you a great nation"; "I will bless you"; "I will make your name great"; "I will bless those who bless you"; "[I will] curse those who curse you" (vv. 2, 3). God will fulfill these promises freely and out of goodness. Yes, Abraham must respond. But his response is only to accept the relationship God has offered.

God's covenant with Abraham (Gen 15). House of the Book & Royal Library, The Hague. Public domain.

Although we may at times imagine that our faith depends upon our piety and good works, our religious and moral achievements do not make our relationship with God possible. From the beginning and always, faith remains God's unconditional grace.

(2) A God of Community. Although faith is personal, it is never just about individuals. Abraham is promised offspring. He is called to become the father of a great nation. God often addresses individuals, but God intends to create communities. Throughout the history of faith that began with Abraham, there have always been families, tribes, nations, temples, synagogues, churches, and mosques. God offers faith so that we may be gathered together. God relates to us as a people.

(3) A God of the Journey. Faith in God is a journey. Our relationship with God develops over time and changes as the course of our life turns from one circumstance to another. Implicit in the relationship is the belief that the One who calls us will accompany us as the journey unfolds. Although the twists and turns of life can be disruptive and frightening, faith allows us to believe that God has a plan for our life and intends to bring it to meaningful fulfillment. When God told Abraham to leave Haran, no destination was given, only the command to begin the journey. Only after Abraham traveled for some time did he realize that the Promised Land was the land of Canaan (v. 7). The God who spoke to Abraham is a God who fulfills promises in history, in the changes of life as they emerge. As it was for Abraham, faith is our willingness to journey through life with the confidence that the One whose voice has called us journeys with us.

To summarize, Genesis 12:1-9 demonstrates that from the beginning our relationship with God has been freely initiated by God. The invitation to faith is directed not simply to individuals but to communities that God calls into existence. Our relationship with God unfolds as a journey, a walk with the God who is revealed to us in the changing circumstances of life.

Before we leave Genesis 12:1-9, we should note that this passage includes a promise that moves the relationship with God beyond the family of Abraham: "All the families of the earth will find blessing in you" (v. 3). One way to understand this verse is that all the nations of the earth will be blessed through Abraham. The New Testament understands it this way, asserting that God intended the faith of Abraham to become a blessing for all the world (Acts 3:25; Gal 3:8). Already, here at the very beginning of our faith tradition, is an indication that the faith of one man will not be limited to him and his family but will extend to all families—in other words, all peoples and, indeed, all creation.

Today we embrace this broad, universal perspective. But we also continue to believe in the nearness of the God of the Family, expecting God to care for those closest to us. I served for many years as the pastor of a Catholic parish, and I can testify to the importance of family in the life of faith. Couples came to be married and registered in the parish not only to participate in the sacraments. They came because they believed and hoped that God would guide their families and help their children grow into good and responsible adults. They turned to God regularly in the hope that their children would be healthy, their homes safe, and their relationships life-giving. Although God has promised us more than family, Abraham's hope remains at the core of what we, too, hope for as believers: to live a blessed life in the midst of those who belong to us.

Contemporary Relevance. From the deep richness of Genesis 12:1-9, allow me to suggest two insights relevant to our present lives.

1) *Life is not fixed.* Far too many people find themselves ensnared by life. Their days have become settled and static. It may seem that all the important decisions have already been made. Perhaps their education is completed, a life-partner has been found, the mortgage has been paid off, the children have been raised. Perhaps their career is settled and their friendships established. As time passes, life falls into a predictable routine. New possibilities recede, and a state of dullness becomes the norm. Instead of being stimulated by life, many people find themselves confined by it, bound by the choices that they have made.

The God of Abraham frees us from such constrictions. Because God initiates and guides the journey of faith, God is fundamentally the God of the new. Before God spoke, Abraham may have never considered leaving Haran. There were too many responsibilities, too many worthy commitments already in place. But when God said, "Go," the fixed parameters of Abraham's life were shattered, and his world bloomed with new energy. All who believe with Abraham should know that God can issue a similar call to each of us. Our lives may feel settled and even dull. But at any age or stage of life, God can break into routines that hem us in. And when God speaks, dead ends open, the brittle becomes fresh, and the far-fetched is suddenly within reach.

2) *It is never too late.* Genesis 12:4 tells us that Abraham was 75 years old when he left Haran. At such an age, we would be tempted to expect life to fade, accomplishments to diminish, and even one's personal worth to be questioned. But when God wished to initiate a relationship with humanity, God chose someone who seemed to have his life behind him, saying, "Go! Begin a new relationship between me and the world."

God's action reminds us that it is not our age but God's call that determines our future. There are certainly things we cannot accomplish at 75. We likely cannot win a marathon or undertake a project that requires decades to complete. But even though our energy is less and our lifespan is more limited, we have not lost the ability to serve. Wisdom can be imparted in a few words. Compassion can be extended to those who suffer. The insights, abilities, and resources gained by years of work and personal connections can be directed to causes that promote peace and justice. It is never too late for God to call us—and never too late for us to respond. Whenever believers in their seventies and beyond respond to God's call, they give witness that it has been that way from the beginning. Our faith and hope in God began when a 75-year-old man named Abraham said, "Yes."

Abraham and the God Who Listens to Us and Cares for the Marginalized

Genesis 15:1-21

The Covenant with Abram. [1]Some time after-
ward, the word of the LORD came to Abram in a
vision: Do not fear, Abram! I am your shield; I
will make your reward very great.
[2]But Abram said, "Lord GOD, what can you
give me, if I die childless and have only a servant
of my household, Eliezer of Damascus?" [3]Abram
continued, "Look, you have given me no off-
spring, so a servant of my household will be my
heir." [4]Then the word of the LORD came to him:
No, that one will not be your heir; your own off-
spring will be your heir. [5]He took him outside and
said: Look up at the sky and count the stars, if you
can. Just so, he added, will your descendants be.
[6]Abram put his faith in the LORD, who attributed
it to him as an act of righteousness.
[7]He then said to him: I am the LORD who
brought you from Ur of the Chaldeans to give
you this land as a possession. [8]"Lord GOD," he
asked, "how will I know that I will possess it?"
[9]He answered him: Bring me a three-year-old
heifer, a three-year-old female goat, a three-year-
old ram, a turtledove, and a young pigeon. [10]He
brought him all these, split them in two, and
placed each half opposite the other; but the birds
he did not cut up. [11]Birds of prey swooped down
on the carcasses, but Abram scared them away.
[12]As the sun was about to set, a deep sleep fell
upon Abram, and a great, dark dread descended
upon him.
[13]Then the LORD said to Abram: Know for
certain that your descendants will reside as aliens
in a land not their own, where they shall be en-
slaved and oppressed for four hundred years. [14]But
I will bring judgment on the nation they must
serve, and after this they will go out with great
wealth. [15]You, however, will go to your ancestors
in peace; you will be buried at a ripe old age. [16]In
the fourth generation your descendants will re-
turn here, for the wickedness of the Amorites is
not yet complete.
[17]When the sun had set and it was dark, there
appeared a smoking fire pot and a flaming torch,
which passed between those pieces. [18]On that day
the LORD made a covenant with Abram, saying:
To your descendants I give this land, from the Wadi
of Egypt to the Great River, the Euphrates, [19]the
land of the Kenites, the Kenizzites, the Kad-
monites, [20]the Hittites, the Perizzites, the Rephaim,
[21]the Amorites, the Canaanites, the Girgashites,
and the Jebusites.

Following the flow of events in the book of Genesis, this second interaction between God and Abraham seems to occur in the Promised Land around Hebron (Gen 13:18). But it is possible that this passage, which shows many parallels with Genesis 12:1-9, is a parallel account of Abraham's original call in Mesopotamia. Again, God initiates the relationship, coming to Abraham in a vision (v. 1). The same two promises are given: offspring (vv. 4-5) and land (v. 7). Verses 13-16 show that the promises to Abraham extend to an entire people and that the people will come to know God through a journey in a foreign land.

However, the total grace of God's call is expressed more dramatically in this passage than in Genesis 12:1-9. The drama comes from a detailed description of a covenant ceremony. In the ancient Near East, covenants were agreements made under oath between two parties to engage in or refrain from certain stipulated actions. Covenants were sealed by ceremonies in which animals were cut in half, and those binding themselves to the covenant would walk between the severed parts. This action expressed the willingness of the parties to experience the same fate as the animals if they broke the agreement. In an action that is unique in the history of religions, God is bound to Abraham by submitting to this ancient rite. Represented by a smoking fire pot and a flaming torch, God passes between the severed animals (vv. 17-18). Abraham himself does not pass between the animal parts. He only watches. The text thereby asserts that the promises to Abraham are unilateral. The relationship with God is God's free gift.

The English word **"covenant"** comes from the Latin *convenire*, which means "to come together." It describes two or more parties coming together to make a contract or agreement. In religious terms, "covenant" expresses the relationship God has established with us.

Characteristics of God. Similar to Genesis 12:1-9, this passage from Genesis 15:1-21 affirms that the God who called Abraham is *a God who freely initiates, a God of community,* and *a God of the journey.* But Genesis 15:1-21 also reveals two more characteristics of our relationship with God.

(4) A God Who Listens. When Abraham heard God's command and promise in Genesis 12:1-4, he said nothing but simply went as God had commanded. But when God promises him reward in Genesis 15:1-21, Abraham speaks. This is the first time Abraham addresses God in the Bible. His words are a complaint! He does not want to hear God speaking of the future when he remains childless. He objects that without his own offspring, he may be forced to designate his servant, Eliezer, as an adoptive son and make him his heir (v. 2). God assures Abraham that this will not be the case and promises descendants as numerous as the stars in the sky (v. 5).

This interchange between God and Abraham reveals for the first time that God is One who listens. God is open to our prayers. This characteristic of God becomes a fundamental element of our relationship with God. In Genesis 18:16-33, for example, Abraham intercedes with God on behalf of Sodom. Moses speaks to God on Mount Sinai (Exod 19:20-25). King David's prayers are collected in the book of Psalms. Hannah, the mother of the prophet Samuel, prays for a son (1 Sam 1:9-19). King Solomon prays for wisdom (1 Kgs 3:4-9). Mary, the mother of Jesus, praises God's goodness (Luke 1:46-56). Jesus pleads with his Father in Gethsemane (Mark 14:32-42). Talking to God is a part of believing. It began with Abraham, who knew that the One who spoke to him would listen.

Abraham is the first of many believers in the Bible who speak to God with intimacy and honesty. His first words to God express blunt disappointment. He shows us that we must pray as the people we are. Human emotions are not only acceptable in prayer but necessary. Strong feelings and recriminations are not an indication of disrespect but of intimacy. We are polite to strangers, but we are brutally honest with those closest to us. Strong emotions, even negative ones, indicate that we care enough to feel. Only a close relationship can risk such passion. God expects and listens for such honest truth.

(5) A God of the Marginalized. In verse 13, God tells Abraham that his descendants will be "aliens in a land not their own." This description anticipates the experience of the Israelite people in Egypt before the exodus. But it also refers to Abraham himself. We have already noted that Abraham's family migrated from Ur of the Chaldeans to Haran (Gen 11:31). Abraham then traveled to Canaan (12:5), Egypt (12:10), and then back to Canaan at Hebron (13:18). His life was that of a wanderer. When Sarah died, Abraham bought a burial site from the Hittites, saying, "Although I am a resident alien among you, sell me from your holdings a burial place, that I may bury my deceased wife" (23:4). Although Abraham had considerable wealth, he did not have his own land. His life was one of moving from place to place, always at the margins of society, distinct from the native populace. One of Israel's earliest confessions of faith captures this nomadic condition, beginning: "My father was a refugee Aramean who went down to Egypt with a

small household and lived there as a resident alien" (Deut 26:5).

It was to this marginalized refugee that God first spoke. Our faith tradition did not begin with God addressing a great king or a vested landowner. God spoke to Abraham, a wandering stranger in a foreign land, a nomad living on the fringes of disparate cities. From the first time God spoke, our God was a God of the vulnerable and the homeless, extending special care for the poor and the powerless. Centuries later, Jesus embraced this truth in a definitive way, insisting that our faith in God is identified with our service to the least among us (Matt 25:40). To this day, our faith insists that we are judged by how we treat the most vulnerable members of society.

Genesis 17:1-14, which recounts an encounter between God and Abraham when he is 99 years old, is very likely a **third version** of Abraham's original call. As in the first two, God initiates and freely establishes the relationship as a gift. The promise is also the same: offspring (17:2) and land (17:8). And, as in Genesis 12:3, a hope larger than Abraham's family is suggested when he is called "the father of a multitude of nations" (17:4).

In a study about faith, we cannot leave this crucial passage of Genesis without discussing its most famous statement. When Abraham questions God about his offspring, God shows him the stars of the sky, saying that his descendants will be just as numerous. Then the text describes Abraham's response: "Abram put his faith in the Lord, who attributed it to him as an act of righteousness" (v. 6). Abraham moves from doubt to trust in the promise. This is a classic description of faith in the Scriptures. Paul cites it as he describes the meaning of faith to both the Galatians (3:6) and the Romans (4:3).

This verse perfectly captures our understanding of faith as entering into and clinging to a relationship with God. How does Abraham move from doubt to belief? The sign God provides for Abraham is the stars in the sky. But stars in themselves prove nothing. How could they convince Abraham that he would have offspring? Perhaps, gazing into the night sky, Abraham saw the vastness of the world around him. The stars—which cannot be counted—were beyond his ability to understand or control. So too was the One who made the promise. Standing transfixed under the heavens, Abraham came to understand that the promise of God could not be proven or fully understood. Faith meant submitting to the Promise-Maker. So Abraham believed in the promise because he trusted in the One who had called him. And so the story of our faith began.

God, in turn, accepted Abraham's faith, "attribut[ing] it to him as an act of righteousness" (v. 6). Subsequent tradition has dissected the theological meaning of "righteousness." Here we only need to understand it biblically. In the Bible, righteousness denotes a proper relationship with God. The righteous person is in good standing with God. God offers a relationship; Abraham accepts it. God presents a promise; Abraham trusts in it. Faith and hope work together. When they do, Abraham is righteous.

Jacob, Esau, and the God Who Reconciles

Another dimension of faith and hope in the God of the Family is revealed in the story of two brothers, Esau and Jacob. Children of the patriarch Isaac and the matriarch Rebekah, Esau and Jacob come from a family that is broken and dysfunctional. The two brothers fight with each other even in their mother's womb (Gen 25:19-26).

The family is divided by favoritism. Isaac's favorite son is Esau, and Rebekah's favorite is Jacob (25:27-28). Although Esau is the firstborn, Jacob maneuvers Esau into selling him his birthright (25:29-34). Then, as Isaac lies dying, Jacob tricks his father into giving him the blessing intended for Esau, thereby becoming the son of the inheritance (27:1-40). Jacob's dishonesty devastates the family. "Esau bore a grudge against Jacob because of the blessing his father had given him. Esau said to himself, 'Let the time of mourning for my father come, so that I may kill my brother Jacob' " (27:41). Jacob must flee for his life.

Decades pass. Jacob marries Leah and Rachel and has twelve children. He decides to return to the Promised Land. There he knows he will again meet his brother. In light of their past history, Jacob does not know what Esau's attitude toward him will be. So Jacob sends envoys to Esau to find out. The envoys return with the message: "We found your brother Esau. He is now coming to meet you, and four hundred men are with him" (32:7). The brother who promised to kill Jacob is now approaching with an army. Jacob is frightened and sends gifts ahead of him, thinking, "If I first appease him with a gift that precedes me, then later, when I face him, perhaps he will forgive me" (32:21). Yet it is far from clear whether Esau will forgive Jacob. So Jacob waits in fear, concerned that his meeting with Esau will be the violent confrontation his dishonesty deserves.

Then, on the night before their meeting, Jacob encounters a mysterious adversary at the Jabbok River (32:23-33). The two wrestle until dawn, and Jacob extracts a blessing from the stranger. Jacob names the place Peniel, meaning "face of God," saying, "I have seen God face to face, . . . yet my life has been spared" (32:31). These words indicate that Jacob believes God was the adversary with whom he struggled.

No sooner does Jacob emerge from the night's ordeal than he sees Esau approaching with his troops. Their dramatic meeting is described in Genesis 33:

Genesis 33:1-11

Jacob and Esau Meet. [1]Jacob looked up and
saw Esau coming, and with him four hundred
men. So he divided his children among Leah, Ra-
chel, and the two maidservants, [2]putting the
maidservants and their children first, Leah and
her children next, and Rachel and Joseph last. [3]He
himself went on ahead of them, bowing to the
ground seven times, until he reached his brother.
[4]Esau ran to meet him, embraced him, and fling-
ing himself on his neck, kissed him as he wept.
[5]Then Esau looked up and saw the women and
children and asked, "Who are these with you?"
Jacob answered, "They are the children with
whom God has graciously favored your servant."
[6]Then the maidservants and their children came
forward and bowed low; [7]next, Leah and her chil-
dren came forward and bowed low; lastly, Joseph
and Rachel came forward and bowed low. [8]Then
Esau asked, "What did you intend with all those
herds that I encountered?" Jacob answered, "It
was to gain my lord's favor." [9]Esau replied, "I have
plenty; my brother, you should keep what is
yours." [10]"No, I beg you!" said Jacob. "If you will
do me the favor, accept this gift from me, since to
see your face is for me like seeing the face of
God—and you have received me so kindly. [11]Ac-
cept the gift I have brought you. For God has been
generous toward me, and I have an abundance."
Since he urged him strongly, Esau accepted.

The first three verses of this passage continue the fearful tension that has been building as the two brothers prepare to meet. With four hundred men accompanying him, Esau's intentions are unclear. For protection, Jacob divides his family, placing his favorite wife and son (Rachel and Joseph) the furthest away from Esau. Jacob then approaches Esau, bowing seven times to indicate his complete submission. He is humbled but still completely vulnerable to what Esau will do.

In a sudden turn, verse 4 reveals that the reaction of Esau is complete forgiveness. Running to Jacob, Esau embraces and kisses him as he weeps. This is the same man who was twice cheated by his younger brother and who had vowed to kill him. Now there is no mention of the past, no words of recrimination, only abounding generosity and joyful reunion. Esau even tries to refuse the gifts from Jacob saying, "I have plenty; my brother, you should keep what is yours" (v. 9).

There is no preparation for such kindness. This text surprises us with its overwhelming forgiveness and thereby suggests that forces beyond Esau's own goodness are at work. The forces are those of God. Jacob tells his brother, "[T]o see your face is for me like seeing the face of God" (v. 10). His statement artfully ties this scene with the one before it at the Jabbok. Just as God was present in the mysterious struggle by the river, God is now visible in the face of a reconciled brother. Just as Jacob survived the encounter with the stranger, he also survives his meeting with Esau. God has been at work, reconciling the estranged brothers.

Characteristics of God. This dramatic narrative not only addresses the healing between Jacob and Esau, but it also establishes another characteristic of God.

(6) A God Who Reconciles. The story of Jacob and Esau reveals to us a God who brings peace and harmony to our relationships. God not only promises offspring to Abraham and his descendants but remains present and active with them, uniting and reuniting their families. Our God is a God of reconciliation. This characteristic of God continues throughout the Bible. It is repeated in the story of Joseph, who is reconciled to his brothers (Gen 37–50). In the New Testament, the parable of the Prodigal Son further testifies to God's power to heal families. The father in the parable, mirroring the actions of Esau, runs to, embraces, and kisses his wayward son (Luke 15:20). From the beginning of our faith tradition, then, God is revealed to us as One who not only gives us families but strives to keep them together.

In this lesson, we have examined how our faith tradition began with Abraham when he entered into and clung to a relationship with God, who promised him what he hoped for: offspring and land. This is faith and hope in the God of the Family. We also identified six characteristics of the God in whom we believe and hope: *(1) A God Who Freely Initiates*, *(2) A God of Community*, *(3) A God of the Journey*, *(4) A God Who Listens*, *(5) A God of the Marginalized*, and *(6) A God Who Reconciles*. All six of these characteristics continue as part of our faith tradition today. The God who first spoke to Abraham is the same God in whom we as Christians continue to believe and hope.

EXPLORING LESSON ONE

1. How would you define faith, hope, and love in your own words?

2. How is our understanding of faith, hope, and love influenced by our understanding of who God is and what God does?

3. How are faith and hope connected with each another?

4. How does God's promise to Abraham in Genesis 12:1-9 reveal God as the God of the Family?

5. The commentary suggests that Abraham was willing to believe in God's promises because they addressed the deepest desire of his and Sarah's hearts. Does this explanation resonate with you? Has God ever given you such a promise?

6. In what way does the second interaction between God and Abraham (Gen 15:1-21) demonstrate that God's promise of land and offspring is a completely free gift, with nothing required from Abraham?

7. Would you characterize your faith as faith in a God who listens? When have you experienced God listening? Have you ever felt that God was not listening?

8. Read Galatians 3:6-9, where Paul quotes Genesis 15:6 and explains that "those who have faith" are "children of Abraham." After reading these passages from Genesis and Galatians, what does it mean to you to be a "child of Abraham"?

9. Jacob sees the face of God both in a time of struggle and in a moment of family reconciliation (Gen 32:23-33; 33:1-11). Can you think of a time in your life when God has been revealed as a God of reconciliation after a time of struggle? How has this experience shaped your faith and hope in God going forward?

10. What insight about faith or hope can you share with your group after studying and reflecting on these stories from Genesis?

CLOSING PRAYER

Prayer

All the families of the earth will find blessing in you. (Gen 12:3)

God of faith and hope, we thank you for our ancestor in faith, Abraham, who listened to your call and placed his trust in you. Grant us the faith and hope of Abraham, so we too may go wherever you call us. Today we pray especially for . . .

LESSON TWO

Faith and Hope in the God of the Nations

Begin your personal study and group discussion with a simple and sincere prayer such as:

Prayer

Lord God, help us listen with the ears of our hearts as we spend time with your word. Reveal yourself to us today as you have revealed yourself through the ages, and strengthen in us your gifts of faith, hope, and love.

Read pages 28–37, Lesson Two.

Respond to the questions on pages 38–40, Exploring Lesson Two.

The Closing Prayer on page 40 is for your personal use and may be used at the end of group discussion.

FAITH AND HOPE IN THE GOD OF THE NATIONS

The Centrality of the Exodus

The most significant event of Israel's faith journey with God is the exodus from Egypt. The book of Genesis ends with Jacob's son Joseph ruling as "lord of all Egypt" (Gen 45:9) and the extended family of Abraham living in peace and prosperity. But the book of Exodus begins by telling us: "Then a new king, who knew nothing of Joseph, rose to power in Egypt" (Exod 1:8). With this development, the descendants of Abraham lose their place of privilege and become one of several foreign groups living under the rule of Pharaoh and working in servitude amid the wealth of Egypt.

Ancient Egyptian records indicate that every so often a people or clan decided to leave Egypt for what they hoped would be a better life. Sometimes the pharaoh would attempt to stop them, and other times he would allow them to fend for themselves in the Sinai wilderness. Early in the rule of Pharaoh Ramses II, around 1290 BCE, the Israelites attempted to leave Egypt. Although Egyptian soldiers pursued them, these descendants of Abraham were able to escape into the desert.

In the late nineteenth century, a series of clay tablets were found in upper Egypt containing correspondence between the Egyptian administration and its representatives in Canaan (present day Israel). Dating from 1400–1375 BCE, the **Amarna Letters** include requests to the pharaoh for help against raiders and nomadic groups who they called *hapiru.* The letters provide a historical context for the early biblical period as a time of unrest when small wandering groups could challenge established political states. The descendants of Abraham who left Egypt in the exodus might be seen as such a group. It has even been suggested that the word "Hebrew" derives from *hapiru.*

What makes Israel's departure from Egypt unique is Israel's interpretation of the event. For the descendants of Abraham, their exodus was not due to chance or their own abilities. It was the work of the God of the Family, who had promised them their own land. Pharaoh was defeated—and they were saved from his wrath—by the God of Abraham.

The exodus marks an important shift in Israel's understanding of God. God is revealed as more than the God of the Family who provides offspring and land. The God of the exodus stands on a world stage, greater than the pharaoh of Egypt and able to defeat him. Because of the exodus, faith becomes believing in and clinging to the One who not only nurtures and cares for families but also controls world events. Hope increases proportionally. Faith in God now directly leads to the hope that God can direct the powers of the world for Israel's benefit. In the exodus, the God of the Family is revealed as the God of the Nations.

The escape from Egypt cannot be separated from what follows it. The scriptural tradition tells the exodus story in three phases: the deliverance from Egypt, the covenant at Sinai, and the entry into the Promised Land. This lesson will discuss our faith and hope in the God of the Nations in three corresponding sections: Out of Egypt, The Covenant at Sinai, and Israel in the Land.

Out of Egypt: The God Who Saves

The exodus from Egypt begins with the call of Moses:

Exodus 3:1-15

[1]Meanwhile Moses was tending the flock of his
father-in-law Jethro, the priest of Midian. Leading
the flock beyond the wilderness, he came to the
mountain of God, Horeb. [2]There the angel of the
LORD appeared to him as fire flaming out of a
bush. When he looked, although the bush was on
fire, it was not being consumed. [3]So Moses de-
cided, "I must turn aside to look at this remarkable
sight. Why does the bush not burn up?" [4]When
the LORD saw that he had turned aside to look,
God called out to him from the bush: Moses!
Moses! He answered, "Here I am." [5]God said: Do
not come near! Remove your sandals from your
feet, for the place where you stand is holy ground.
[6]I am the God of your father, he continued, the
God of Abraham, the God of Isaac, and the God
of Jacob. Moses hid his face, for he was afraid to
look at God.
The Call and Commission of Moses. [7]But the
LORD said: I have witnessed the affliction of my
people in Egypt and have heard their cry against
their taskmasters, so I know well what they are
suffering. [8]Therefore I have come down to rescue
them from the power of the Egyptians and lead
them up from that land into a good and spacious
land, a land flowing with milk and honey, the
country of the Canaanites, the Hittites, the Amor-
ites, the Perizzites, the Girgashites, the Hivites and
the Jebusites. [9]Now indeed the outcry of the Isra-
elites has reached me, and I have seen how the
Egyptians are oppressing them. [10]Now, go! I am
sending you to Pharaoh to bring my people, the
Israelites, out of Egypt.
[11]But Moses said to God, "Who am I that I
should go to Pharaoh and bring the Israelites out
of Egypt?" [12]God answered: I will be with you;
and this will be your sign that I have sent you.
When you have brought the people out of Egypt,
you will serve God at this mountain. [13]"But," said
Moses to God, "if I go to the Israelites and say to
them, 'The God of your ancestors has sent me to
you,' and they ask me, 'What is his name?' what
do I tell them?" [14]God replied to Moses: I am who
I am. Then he added: This is what you will tell the
Israelites: I AM has sent me to you.
[15]God spoke further to Moses: This is what you
will say to the Israelites: The LORD, the God of
your ancestors, the God of Abraham, the God of
Isaac, and the God of Jacob, has sent me to you.

This is my name forever;
this is my title for all generations.

The first thing to notice about this famous passage of the burning bush is that the God who addresses Moses is not a new God. The text emphasizes continuity with the God of Abraham, Isaac, and Jacob (vv. 6, 15). This is the God of the Family who is about to be revealed as the God of the Nations.

The promise of the land made to Abraham also remains in place: Israel will receive "a good and spacious" territory "flowing with milk and honey" (v. 8). God continues to display the characteristics first revealed in the early narratives of the patriarchs and matriarchs. As in the promise made to Abraham, God *freely initiates* the exodus without conditions: "I have come down to rescue them from the power of the Egyptians" (v. 8). As with Abraham, God *listens*: "Now indeed the outcry of the Israelites has reached me" (v. 9). And just as God first spoke to Abraham when Abraham was a refugee wanderer, God continues to *care for the marginalized* and powerless by leading the enslaved Israelites out of oppression in Egypt.

What is new in this passage is the revelation of God's name. Names in the Bible are not mere tags to distinguish one person from another. Names are meant to capture the essence of a person. "What is your name?" really means "Who are you?" Asking God's name is asking God to reveal God's true identity.

When Moses requests God's name, he receives more than he asks for. He is given two names. Verse 14 says that God's name is "I am who I am," or simply "I AM." Verse 15 says that God's name is "[t]he LORD." Let's begin with the second name. "Lord" in Hebrew is *Adonai.* It is not a name but a title. After the exile, God's personal name ("YHWH" in the Hebrew text) was considered too holy to pronounce. So as Jews read the biblical text, they substituted the title *Adonai* ("Lord") wherever the name "YHWH" occurred. This practice has continued in our English translations wherever you see the title "Lord" printed with small capitals as "LORD."

God's personal name consists of four Hebrew letters: YHWH (formally called the **tetragrammaton**—meaning "four letters"). Although it was once popular to use a vocalization of the tetragrammaton ("Yahweh") in some liturgical music, a 2008 Vatican instruction directed that this should be avoided because of the longstanding Jewish-Christian practice of not audibly speaking God's personal name.

Therefore, behind "[t]he LORD" in verse 15 is really God's personal name ("YHWH"). The origins of this name are ancient, and its exact meaning eludes us. This may be why the authors of Exodus provided another name in verse 14: "I am who I am." But this name is also elusive. It can be translated in widely different ways. In addition to "I am who I am," the Hebrew could also mean "I am what I am," "I will be who I will be," "I am that I am," "I cause to be what is," and "I am the One who endures." Perhaps the strategy of this name is to keep God's identity a mystery.

Nevertheless, if we must choose, "I will be who I will be" is an especially plausible construction of the Hebrew, and this option corresponds to a characteristic we have already associated with God: *a God of the journey*. With the name "I will be who I will be," God is telling Moses that he will never know God's inner being but that he will come to know God as they journey together over time. As the Israelites experience God's presence and guidance, they will come to understand who God is. They will come to know God's name.

After the encounter at the burning bush, Moses accepts God's call and goes to Pharaoh. A contest then takes place between Moses and Pharaoh's magicians (Exod 7:8-13), and ten plagues are sent by God (7:14–12:30). These events demonstrate that the God of the Nations is more powerful than the pharaoh. Pharaoh finally allows the Israelites to leave Egypt (12:31-32), only to later change his mind and pursue them with horses and chariots (14:5-9). This sets up the ultimate confrontation between God and Pharaoh at the Red Sea.

The crossing of the Red Sea is the focal event of the exodus. Here the biblical authors have woven together several strains of tradition to enrich the meaning of the narrative. Above all, the exodus displays God's power and supremacy over the armies of Egypt—and indeed over all human forces. This becomes clear as the Israelites complain to God and Moses:

Exodus 14:10-14

Crossing the Red Sea. 10Now Pharaoh was near when the Israelites looked up and saw that the Egyptians had set out after them. Greatly frightened, the Israelites cried out to the LORD. 11To Moses they said, "Were there no burial places in Egypt that you brought us to die in the wilderness? What have you done to us, bringing us out of Egypt? 12Did we not tell you this in Egypt, when we said, 'Leave us alone that we may serve the Egyptians'? Far better for us to serve the Egyptians than to die in the wilderness." 13But Moses answered the people, "Do not fear! Stand your ground and see the victory the LORD will win for you today. For these Egyptians whom you see today you will never see again. 14The LORD will fight for you; you have only to keep still."

The exodus is not accomplished through the power or faith of the Israelites. Cowering in fear, they are ready to go back to Egypt. Rather, the exodus is a mighty act of God. It is Moses who provides this interpretation through the eyes of faith. He insists that the fearsome Egyptian army descending upon the Israelites will be an opportunity for God's victory. The Israelites do not need to act or even believe, just stand still (v. 14).

The text then describes God's supremacy:

Exodus 14:21-31

[21]Then Moses stretched out his hand over the
sea; and the LORD drove back the sea with a strong
east wind all night long and turned the sea into dry
ground. The waters were split, [22]so that the Israelites
entered into the midst of the sea on dry land, with
the water as a wall to their right and to their left.
Rout of the Egyptians. [23]The Egyptians fol-
lowed in pursuit after them—all Pharaoh's horses
and chariots and horsemen—into the midst of the
sea. [24]But during the watch just before dawn, the
LORD looked down from a column of fiery cloud
upon the Egyptian army and threw it into a panic;
[25]and he so clogged their chariot wheels that they
could drive only with difficulty. With that the
Egyptians said, "Let us flee from Israel, because
the LORD is fighting for them against Egypt."
[26]Then the LORD spoke to Moses: Stretch out
your hand over the sea, that the water may flow
back upon the Egyptians, upon their chariots and
their horsemen. [27]So Moses stretched out his hand
over the sea, and at daybreak the sea returned to
its normal flow. The Egyptians were fleeing head
on toward it when the LORD cast the Egyptians
into the midst of the sea. [28]As the water flowed
back, it covered the chariots and the horsemen.
Of all Pharaoh's army which had followed the Is-
raelites into the sea, not even one escaped. [29]But
the Israelites had walked on dry land through the
midst of the sea, with the water as a wall to their
right and to their left. [30]Thus the LORD saved Israel
on that day from the power of Egypt. When Israel
saw the Egyptians lying dead on the seashore [31]and
saw the great power that the LORD had shown
against Egypt, the people feared the LORD. They
believed in the LORD and in Moses his servant.

Consistent with Moses' word, the people play no role in God's victory. They only walk across the sea on dry land once God's action is complete (v. 29). When Israel sees the great power God has displayed, they believe in the Lord and in Moses, God's servant (v. 31). Faith, then, is not a prerequisite for God's action but a response to it. Witnessing God's power over Pharaoh, the Israelites now believe in the One who rules the nations. They accept Moses' interpretation: Their God has saved them.

The Death of the Egyptians

The narrative of the exodus exalts in God's saving action on behalf of Israel. But what about the Egyptians who were left dead on the seashore? Are we to understand that God destroys some people for the sake of others?

Such a conclusion pushes the story too far. The point of the exodus story is that God saves Israel, not that God destroys Egyptians. Yet the death of the Egyptians remains problematic and was not overlooked by later Jewish interpreters. To address this difficulty in the text, they offered a story in which God forbids the angels in heaven to rejoice over Israel's crossing of the Red Sea, saying to them, "This is no time to sing when My creatures, human beings whom I made, are drowning!" (*Sanhedrin* 39b).

There is no joy in heaven over the death of anyone God has made.

Characteristics of God. The crossing of the Red Sea crystallizes another characteristic of God that is present throughout Scripture.

(7) A God Who Saves. For the Jewish people, the exodus is the premier revelation of God as savior. Just as Christians ground their faith in the death and resurrection of Jesus, Jews draw upon the exodus to understand who God is.

In the exodus, faith in God becomes faith in a God who can and does control the events of history. Hope becomes trusting that God will save God's people from whatever political or natural forces may threaten or harm them. No longer only the God of the Family, God is now understood as the God of the Nations who rules the world and everything in it. As God says to Moses: "[A]ll the earth is mine" (Exod 19:5).

Contemporary Relevance. It is commonplace for us to understand that God's saving power extends to every aspect of our world. This belief was first revealed in the exodus. But the narrative of the crossing of the Red Sea also provides an opportunity to reflect on *how* God's power is experienced. The biblical text clearly asserts that God saved Israel. However, the presentation of God's action is complicated. Multiple sources have been joined to create this famous passage. As a result, Exodus 14:21-31 contains two different pictures of how the deliverance of Israel took place.

There is a *miraculous* presentation in which the sea is split, creating a path between two great walls of water (vv. 21c-22, 29). Israel crosses on this dry path, and when the Egyptians follow, the walls of water fall upon them and drown them all (vv. 28-29). But the same narrative also includes a *natural* presentation in which the Lord causes the water to be driven back by a strong east wind that blows all night and dries the ground (v. 21a-b). The Israelites are able to cross, but the Egyptian's chariot wheels become clogged (v. 25a). At daybreak the sea returns to its normal flow, and all the Egyptians are drowned (v. 27).

The biblical account of the crossing of the Red Sea allows us to see God miraculously contravening the laws of nature. But it also shows God using natural forces for divine purpose. This difference mirrors God's action in our lives today. Sometimes we experience God's power in a dramatic manner that cannot be explained. A malignant cancer suddenly disappears. We wake from a sound sleep just in time to save our infant son from danger. At other times we see God acting through commonplace occurrences. A friend convinces us to go out for a beer, and we meet our future spouse. We go to college determined to attain a law degree, but while there we take an elective on theater arts that so moves our soul that we decide to pursue an acting career.

As people of faith, we believe that God is always working in our lives. Sometimes God's power moves through everyday circumstances. Other times it is inexplicable and miraculous. God can act with subtlety and coincidence. But God is still free to strike with thunder.

The Covenant at Sinai: The God Who Expects Moral Action and Forgives

The book of Exodus moves quickly from the Red Sea to Mount Sinai. By chapter 19 the Israelites have arrived at the holy mountain. The last twenty-two chapters of Exodus (19–40), all of the book of Leviticus, and the first ten chapters of the book of Numbers describe a single stay at Sinai where God makes a covenant with Israel.

The space the Bible devotes to this covenant underscores its importance. We will limit our discussion of the Sinai covenant to three passages. The first two (Exod 19:3-8 and 24:3-8) frame an early body of laws (Exod 20–23). These two passages will allow us to explore the role of law in Israel's relationship with God. The third passage (Exod 34:5-9) describes the renewal of the covenant after Israel's apostasy with the golden calf.

We begin with the first passage:

Exodus 19:3-8

[3]Moses went up to the mountain of God. Then the LORD called to him from the mountain, saying: This is what you will say to the house of Jacob; tell the Israelites: [4]You have seen how I treated the Egyptians and how I bore you up on

eagles' wings and brought you to myself. 5Now, if
you obey me completely and keep my covenant,
you will be my treasured possession among all
peoples, though all the earth is mine. 6You will be
to me a kingdom of priests, a holy nation. That is
what you must tell the Israelites. 7So Moses went
and summoned the elders of the people. When
he set before them all that the LORD had ordered
him to tell them, 8all the people answered to-
gether, "Everything the LORD has said, we will
do." Then Moses brought back to the LORD the
response of the people.

Here, at the foot of Mount Sinai, the people of Israel agree to do all that God commands them. God's saving action in the exodus grounds Israel's faith (v. 4) and enables the people to accept God's directives (v. 8). This biblical text describes the people agreeing to God's commands even before any laws are enumerated. Just as Abraham left Haran solely on the word of the One who called him, the Israelites accept the law because of the One who gives it. Faith is clinging unconditionally to the One who is revealed. Therefore, the Israelites already know that they will obey whatever God asks. The personal relationship precedes obedience to commands.

The God of the Nations gives Israel a special role among the nations. They are to be God's "treasured possession," "a kingdom of priests, a holy nation" (vv. 5-6). This new status is one of service. As God's treasured possession, Israel is to become God's instrument to carry out God's purpose. As priests, they are servants rather than rulers, mediating between God and other kingdoms. As a holy nation, Israel is set apart not simply *from* other nations but *for* other nations, to bring about God's purposes in the world.

Contemporary Relevance. Those who believe in a God who rules the nations are inescapably called to serve the nations. The New Testament specifically applies the servant role of Israel to the followers of Jesus: "But you are 'a chosen race, a royal priesthood, a holy nation, a people of his own, so that you may announce the praises' of him who called you out of darkness into his wonderful light" (1 Pet 2:9). If our God were only the God of the Family, our love and service could be limited to those closest to us. But once we believe in God as the ruler of all the earth, then worldwide concerns become our concerns. Economic injustice between nations, military aggression between peoples, evils resulting from racism, unfair policies of immigration, and violation of the earth's environment all become religious issues that call for our involvement. All who profess faith and hope in God must work for God's will to be done on earth.

The book of Exodus continues with God giving the Ten Commandments (Exod 20) and an early body of laws called the Covenant Code (Exod 21–23). Exodus 24 then presents a covenant ceremony in which Israel agrees to follow God's commands:

Exodus 24:3-8

Ratification of the Covenant. 1Moses himself
was told: Come up to the LORD, you and Aaron,
with Nadab, Abihu, and seventy of the elders of
Israel. You shall bow down at a distance. 2Moses
alone is to come close to the LORD; the others
shall not come close, and the people shall not
come up with them.

3When Moses came to the people and related
all the words and ordinances of the LORD, they all
answered with one voice, "We will do everything
that the LORD has told us." 4Moses then wrote
down all the words of the LORD and, rising early
in the morning, he built at the foot of the moun-
tain an altar and twelve sacred stones for the
twelve tribes of Israel. 5 Then, having sent young
men of the Israelites to offer burnt offerings and
sacrifice young bulls as communion offerings to
the LORD, 6Moses took half of the blood and put

continue

> it in large bowls; the other half he splashed on the altar. [7]Taking the book of the covenant, he read it aloud to the people, who answered, "All that the LORD has said, we will hear and do." [8]Then he took the blood and splashed it on the people, saying, "This is the blood of the covenant which the LORD has made with you according to all these words."

The relationship of this passage to Exodus 19:3-8 is evident. In 24:7, the people agree to God's commands ("All that the LORD has said, we will hear and do"), echoing their assent in 19:8. The difference is that, in this passage, they now know the actual commands of the Lord that they are to follow. These commands are representative of all the commandments of God. The biblical authors have located all of Israel's legislation, from whatever age, on Mount Sinai. Even laws that developed centuries later when Israel was in the land or during the Israelite monarchy are included as part of Israel's covenant ceremony on the holy mountain.

This historical realignment has profound religious meaning. Any law in Israel gains its authority not from the tribe who devises it or the king who promulgates it but from its connection to the covenant relationship with God. Because of this already-established and unconditional bond, Israel follows the commandments of God. The laws do not create the relationship. Rather, keeping God's commands is a way of living it. Following God's law gives witness that Israel belongs to God.

Characteristics of God. The giving of the law to Israel reveals an eighth characteristic of God.

(8) A God Who Expects Moral Action. Believing in and clinging to God cannot remain an interior disposition. Faith must be expressed outwardly in moral action. Therefore, God gives the law as a guide for the kind of life that must characterize the believer. The gift of the law stands contrary to every view that holiness is passivity of the soul or the suppression of human effort so that God can act for us. In fact, the law displays God's desire to involve humans in God's saving plan. Always holding God as the primary agent, the law insists that there are important moral initiatives and responsibilities that must be undertaken. God's chosen people are called to support and advance God's will for creation by doing what is right.

Neither are the commands of the law arbitrary. The demands of the law mirror what God has done and what God considers important. The Ten Commandments (Exod 20:1-17) and other early laws command action that is necessary for peace and justice within society. Particularly relevant are the laws supporting the care for the poor and marginalized. Mercy is to be extended to them because God showed mercy to Israel: "You shall not oppress or afflict a resident alien, for you were once aliens residing in the land of Egypt. You shall not wrong any widow or orphan. If ever you wrong them and they cry out to me, I will surely listen to their cry" (Exod 22:20-23; see also 23:9). God's concern for the marginalized, first revealed to Abraham, is now entrusted to human beings and enshrined in divine law.

Contemporary Relevance. The Jewish understanding of law has been often misrepresented in Christian theology. Jews have been frequently presented as blindly following the law to earn salvation. Judaism has been falsely understood as a religion of legalism, a human effort to force or control the hand of God. This misconception has been supported by a false reading of Paul's letters. Paul's occasional criticisms of the law were understood as a result of his frustration at being unable to follow the demands of the law and thereby stand in good relationship with God. Christian interpreters employed this misleading perspective to assert that the essence of Jesus' teaching was freedom from the law. But the law is not a burden from which we must be freed. The Hebrew Scriptures present a healthy appreciation of God's commands: We are called to obey, but we are saved by God's free gift.

Christians believe that our relationship with God in Christ is solely based on God's gift. This is not a departure from but a continuation of the Jewish tradition. From the time of Abraham, our relationship with God has been one of entering into and clinging to a relationship that is freely given. We do not stand in this relationship because we obey God's commands. Rather, we obey God's commands because we stand in this relationship. Not only Christians but also Jews accept the primacy of God's unmerited grace. What separates Jews and Christians is a disagreement not over the role of the law but over the identification of Jesus as the Christ.

A profound irony in the book of Exodus is that no sooner do the Israelites accept the Covenant of Sinai than they break it. Even as Moses remains on the mountain with God, the Israelites fashion a calf out of gold and worship it (32:1-6). They thereby disobey the first of the Ten Commandments: to worship God alone (20:2-6). When he sees the people dancing before the golden calf, Moses destroys the tablets on which God had written the commandments (32:19). God is inclined to destroy Israel and make a new people from the descendants of Moses (32:10). But Moses intercedes for Israel by reminding God of the promises made to Abraham, and God relents (32:13-14). Moses cuts two stone tablets so God can rewrite the commandments (34:1-4). The covenant is then renewed:

Exodus 34:5-9

[5]The LORD came down in a cloud and stood
with him there and proclaimed the name, "LORD."
[6]So the LORD passed before him and proclaimed:
The LORD, the LORD, a God gracious and merciful,
slow to anger and abounding in love and fidelity,
[7]continuing his love for a thousand generations,
and forgiving wickedness, rebellion, and sin; yet
not declaring the guilty guiltless, but bringing punishment for their parents' wickedness on children
and children's children to the third and fourth generation! [8]Moses at once knelt and bowed down to
the ground. [9]Then he said, "If I find favor with you,
Lord, please, Lord, come along in our company.
This is indeed a stiff-necked people; yet pardon our
wickedness and sins, and claim us as your own."

God follows Moses' request and pardons Israel's wickedness and sin. God thereby recommits to a covenant with Israel. God passes before Moses and redefines who God is, presenting again the divine name (v. 5).

At the burning bush, God's name was revealed as "I will be who I will be," an identity that will become clear as history unfolds. And here, in history, it is affirmed that God will be a God of mercy: "The LORD, the LORD, a God gracious and merciful, slow to anger and abounding in love and fidelity, continuing his love for a thousand generations, and forgiving wickedness, rebellion, and sin" (vv. 6-7).

Characteristics of God. This description of God becomes definitive in the Bible and reveals to us another characteristic of God.

(9) A God Who Forgives. The Scriptures frequently extol this description of God's mercy (see Num 14:18; Neh 9:17; Pss 103:8-10, 17; 145:8; Jer 32:18; Nah 1:3) because it captures Israel's experience of God in history. God is the One who freely forgives. Because of human frailty, Israel's promise, "We will do everything that the LORD has told us" (Exod 24:3), is not definitive. But God's mercy *is* definitive. God cannot simply be the God who accepts obedience. God must also be the God who forgives disobedience.

Exodus 34:5-9 presents God as forgiving Israel for breaking the commandments even before they are rewritten on the stone tablets (which takes place at Exod 34:27-28). God is the One who forgives so often that "gracious and merciful" become God's name (v. 6). It is a name that God accepts and calls God's own, for God is willing to show mercy for a thousand generations. Faith, then, is believing in such a God, and hope is expecting that no matter how seriously we have sinned, God will forgive us.

Contemporary Relevance. We cannot believe in the God who forgives if we base our relationship with God on our own goodness. As much as we try to follow all of God's laws, we fall short of what God expects of us. Blessed as we are with friends and possessions, we are still envious of a family member or friend who has something we want. Despite the many

Does God punish children for their parents' sins?

Exodus 34:6-7 is one of several passages in the Bible which seem to indicate that God will punish children for their parents' sins (see also Deut 5:9; Isa 14:21; John 9:2). But other passages speak forcibly against such an understanding, for example: "Only the one who sins shall die. The son shall not be charged with the guilt of his father, nor shall the father be charged with the guilt of his son. Justice belongs to the just, and wickedness to the wicked" (Ezek 18:20; see also Deut 24:16; Jer 31:29-30; Rom 14:12).

How might we resolve these conflicting statements? We can begin by drawing a distinction between accountability and influence. Who is accountable for sin? The person who commits it. This is what Ezekiel asserts. But we also know that the sin of any person influences others, especially those within a person's family. The consequences of selfishness, pride, and abuse can wound a family for years to come.

Perhaps Exodus 34:6-7 points to the reality that, in some cases, the consequences of sin influence generations. Yet the context of this verse and the witness of other passages in Scripture remind us that God's mercy, forgiveness, and healing also continue generation after generation.

times we have repented and confessed a habit of sin, it controls us and pulls us down. Over and over again, a prejudice against those of a different race or sexual orientation leads us to demean others both in private and in social settings. We keep striving for the day we can come to God pure and wholly obedient, but we keep falling back into sin. Perhaps it is time to admit that we will never attain perfection and that God has willingly accepted our inadequacy as part of our relationship.

Our covenant with God is based not on our goodness but on God's mercy. We believe and cling to a God who is willing to forgive us for a thousand generations. We might prefer to come to God on our own terms, wrapped in perfection. But God knows us better than we know ourselves. That is why God comes to us as the God who forgives. Mercy is God's name. It is "who God will be."

Israel in the Land: The God Who Creates

After Sinai, Israel journeys to the land that was once promised to Abraham (a journey recounted in Num 10:11–36:13 and the book of Deuteronomy). The historical books then trace how Israel settles in the land (Joshua and Judges) and lives as a monarchy (1–2 Sam and 1–2 Kgs). Israel now exists as its own kingdom, and its faith is in the God of the Nations.

Characteristics of God. As Israel adopted political institutions similar to the other nations of the ancient Near East, it composed foundational stories that mirrored those of the great civilizations around it. Aware of the creation stories of Sumer and Babylon, Israel produced its own accounts of the beginning of the world, guided by faith and inspired by the Holy Spirit. These stories reveal a tenth characteristic of God.

(10) A God Who Creates. The earliest biblical account of creation is found in Genesis 2 and was most likely written during the monarchies of David and Solomon (1000–922 BCE). The dramatic creation account of Genesis 1 is a later composition, probably dating from the time of the exile (587–538 BCE). But scattered throughout the Bible are many assertions of Israel's belief that God made all things. Psalm 8:4, for example, calls the heavens "the work of [God's] fingers." Psalm 104:5 says that God "fixed the earth on its foundation." Other passages describe God creating through a battle with chaos, often personalized with the name "Leviathan."

A powerful example of this is found in Psalm 74 (see also Isa 27:1; Job 3:8):

Psalm 74:13-17

13 You stirred up the sea by your might;
you smashed the heads of the dragons on the waters.
14 You crushed the heads of Leviathan,
gave him as food to the sharks.
15 You opened up springs and torrents,
brought dry land out of the primeval waters.
16 Yours the day and yours the night too;
you set the moon and sun in place.
17 You fixed all the limits of the earth;
summer and winter you made.

Delivered from Egypt and settled on its own land, Israel had seen God's mighty deeds in history. God's power now extended to the whole earth. From this conviction, it was a logical step to conclude that the One who ruled over all nations had in fact made all things. Through the experience of the exodus, Israel came to know and understand God as creator.

Contemporary Relevance. Of the characteristics of God we have identified up to this point, *a God who creates* is the most concrete. The material world, which we believe God created, not only speaks to our minds and hearts but also to our senses. For example, we believe that *God listens to our prayers*, but that belief is not as tangible as the smell of roses in our garden. We acknowledge that *our God expects moral action*, but that belief does not have the raw power of a summer thunderstorm. We trust that *God journeys with us* through life, but that conviction is not as warm as the newborn daughter who sleeps in our arms.

The material world surrounds us always. When we see it as the work of One who loves us, it can lead us each day to deepen our relationship with the God of Abraham.

In the period of Israel's monarchical rule, Abraham's faith in God was fully vindicated, and Abraham's hope for offspring and land was definitively fulfilled. Abraham's descendants became as numerous as the stars in the heavens and lived on their own land. The God of the Family was now the God of a nation with clear borders. The Israelite kings served as God's agents to rule the nation. Believing in a God who saved them in the exodus and could bend the course of history, Israel could now hope that God would protect their nation from its enemies. The king was seen as God's son, whom God would support militarily against the plotting of other nations (Ps 2).

At the apex of Israel's monarchy, God made a promise to David: "Your house and your kingdom are firm forever before me; your throne shall be firmly established forever" (2 Sam 7:16). The promise to David was unconditional. Like the covenant with Abraham, God simply established a unilateral bond.

In the monarchy, Israel's relationship with God seemed settled. Faith was believing in the God who had honored the promises to Abraham. Hope was trusting that such a fulfillment would endure. Faith was worshipping a God who was both creator and savior in the Jerusalem temple. Hope was expecting the continued rule of an Israelite king on David's throne. Faith was real. Hope was reliable. It appeared that Israel's journey with God was complete.

It was not.

The high point of the **Israelite monarchy** occurred under Kings David and Solomon (1020–930 BCE). At the death of Solomon, the kingdom split into two parts: the northern kingdom of Israel and the southern kingdom of Judah. Each kingdom developed its own emphasis in understanding the covenant with God. The northern kingdom was destroyed by the Assyrian empire in 721 BCE. The southern kingdom continued until two invasions in 598 and 587 BCE led to exile in Babylon.

EXPLORING LESSON TWO

1. How did the exodus from Egypt expand Israel's faith in God?

2. God's name is revealed to Moses as "I am who I am" or, as it is sometimes translated, "I will be who I will be" (Exod 3:14). What does this name say to you about God? How does this name influence your faith and hope?

3. In the account of the crossing of the Red Sea (Exod 14:21-31), God utilizes both supernatural and natural means to save the people of Israel. Have you experienced the power of God working in your life in both ways? Can you share an example of each?

4. The Israelites promise to follow God's laws even before those laws are revealed (Exod 19:7-8). What does this tell you about the nature of their faith?

5. What does it mean for Israel to be God's "treasured possession among all peoples" and "a kingdom of priests, a holy nation" (Exod 19:5-6)?

6. What does the revelation of God as the God of the Nations mean for the way we live out our faith?

7. The Israelites consider living God's law to be a life-giving expression of the covenant relationship with God. Christians experience something similar in following the teachings of Jesus, who said: "If you love me, you will keep my commandments" (John 14:15). How can living God's law/commandments be an expression of faith, hope, and love?

8. After God forgives Israel for worshipping the golden calf, "gracious and merciful" is revealed as essential to God's name and identity (Exod 34:6). How have you experienced God as a forgiving God who is gracious, merciful, slow to anger, and abounding in love? How has this experience strengthened or shaped your faith and hope?

9. How and when did the creation stories of Genesis 1–2 emerge? How do these stories reflect Israel's growing faith and hope in God?

10. What insight about faith or hope can you share with your group after studying and reflecting on these stories from Exodus?

CLOSING PRAYER

Prayer

But Moses answered the people, "Do not fear! Stand your ground and see the victory the LORD *will win for you today. . . . The* LORD *will fight for you; you have only to keep still."* (Exod 14:13-14)

God of faith and hope, you have revealed yourself as a God of action and a God who saves. Increase our faith in your salvation and our hope that you will always care for us. Inspired by this faith and hope, strengthen us in turn to care for others. Today we pray for those who need us most, especially . . .

LESSON THREE

Faith and Hope in the God of the World to Come

Begin your personal study and group discussion with a simple and sincere prayer such as:

Prayer

Lord God, help us listen with the ears of our hearts as we spend time with your word. Reveal yourself to us today as you have revealed yourself through the ages, and strengthen in us your gifts of faith, hope, and love.

Read pages 42–52, Lesson Three.

Respond to the questions on pages 53–55, Exploring Lesson Three.

The Closing Prayer on page 56 is for your personal use and may be used at the end of group discussion.

FAITH AND HOPE IN THE GOD OF THE WORLD TO COME

In 587 BCE, Jerusalem was destroyed. After a thirty-month siege, the walls of the city were breached, and Nebuchadnezzar II, king of the Neo-Babylonian Empire, directed his troops to burn the city to the ground. The temple of Solomon was razed. Zedekiah, the last king to sit on David's throne, was taken captive to Babylon, together with Judah's ruling class and many other Judean citizens. The kingdom of Judah was abolished. Its land was annexed to an existing Babylonian province.

The destruction of Jerusalem devastated Israelite faith and hope. God's people had placed their faith in the God of the Nations, but the nation was now gone. They had hoped in a God who would protect them from harm, but their enemies had reduced their city to rubble. Captives now in a foreign country, the land promised to Abraham was but a memory. Could faith and hope in God continue?

This question was compounded by the people's experience in Babylon. The exiles had a reasonable amount of freedom. They were able to assemble, purchase property, and work in various trades. They could not help but be overwhelmed and amazed by the size and wealth of Babylon. Its gates, towers, and temples far outshone those of Jerusalem. Its grand processions to the Babylonian god, Marduk, surpassed the splendor of worship in Solomon's temple. The grandeur of Babylon continually suggested that, despite Israel's claims that the Lord was creator and ruler of nations, the god of Babylon was greater than the God of Israel. Many of the exiles chose to assimilate into Babylonian culture, worshipping Marduk as their god.

But other exiles searched for a way faith and hope in God could continue. They held fast to their ancestral traditions and preserved the ancient religious scrolls they had carried from Jerusalem. It was not clear, however, whether their relationship with God could be maintained. The Jerusalem temple on Mount Zion where God's praises had been sung for generations lay in ruins. Could God even be addressed in Babylon?

Psalm 137:1-6

1By the rivers of Babylon
there we sat weeping
when we remembered Zion.
2On the poplars in its midst
we hung up our harps.
3For there our captors asked us
for the words of a song;
Our tormentors, for joy:
"Sing for us a song of Zion!"
4But how could we sing a song of the LORD
in a foreign land?
5If I forget you, Jerusalem,
may my right hand forget.
6May my tongue stick to my palate
if I do not remember you,
If I do not exalt Jerusalem
beyond all my delights.

The beginning verses of Psalm 137 present a poetic description of the exiles' dilemma:

Those who wished to continue their relationship with God were determined to remember. But memories of the past were not enough. The question of faith was whether their covenant with God was still tenable, whether it was still realistic to hope. Who do you believe in when you're certain that the one in whom you have placed your faith has failed you? What do you hope for when your hope has been taken away?

The exiles who wished to continue in covenant with God understood that the relationship with God as they had previously known and experienced it—as an independent nation with their own king—had ended. In their new circumstances, they needed to reexamine what God had revealed to them and what God had done for them in order to imagine a new way of living in faith and hope.

In time, a way forward was provided by one of Israel's greatest prophets: Jeremiah.

Jeremiah: A Prophecy of Tearing Down

Israel's kings, like most rulers of the ancient Near East, would regularly consult prophets to discern the divine will before making any major policy decisions. Some prophets were employed by kings for this purpose. Of course, prophets who were a part of royal retinues were more likely to say what kings wanted to hear. Notably, most of the prophets found in the Hebrew Bible did *not* agree with Israel's kings but challenged them. Jeremiah was one of these prophets.

Jeremiah was active as a prophet for forty-five years (627–582 BCE). His most forceful pronouncements occurred in the last days of the kingdom of Judah under the kings Jehoiakim and Zedekiah. God sent Jeremiah to "uproot and to tear down, / to destroy and to demolish, / to build and to plant" (Jer 1:10b). His prophetic mission, then, was both to tear down and to build up. Jeremiah announced the destruction of Jerusalem. But he also planted new seeds of hope.

Jeremiah's prophecy of doom involved a frontal attack upon the prevalent understanding of Israel's relationship with God. That understanding can be appropriately called "royal covenant theology" because it asserted that God had established an irrevocable covenant with Israel through King David. Therefore, despite the political upheavals of the world around it, Israel came to believe that it would never fall to an enemy: The temple in Jerusalem was the house of God, and God would protect the king and the nation from every attack. This theology flowed naturally from several characteristics of God that we have identified in the biblical tradition. *A God who freely initiated* a relationship with Abraham and his descendants, *who saved Israel* in the exodus, and who established a nation in the Promised Land would always remain faithful. The nation would therefore stand forever.

It was Jeremiah's mission to announce that it would not. When King Jehoiakim came to the throne in 609 BCE, he found himself caught between the two great powers of his day: Egypt and Babylon. Jehoiakim played one

Understanding Terms: Hebrews, Israelites, and Jews

Hebrews	A name for the Israelite people most often used by strangers or foreigners (see Exod 1:16; 2:6). "Hebrew" also refers to the language of most of the Old Testament.
Israelites	Descendants of Jacob, whose other name is Israel (Gen 32:29). The common term for God's people until the Babylonian exile in the sixth century BCE.
Judeans/Jews	The common term for the descendants of Jacob during and after the Babylonian exile. The tribe and territory of Judah (southern kingdom) were all that remained of ancient Israel after the Assyrian deportation of the northern tribes in 722 BCE.

empire off the other in an attempt to keep his kingdom secure. His political strategies were supported by the royal covenant theology that assured him he would not fail. But Jeremiah attacked this theology. His most famous sermon, given in the Jerusalem temple early in Jehoiakim's reign, is found in Jeremiah 7:

Jeremiah 7:1-15

The Temple Sermon. 1The word came to Jer-
emiah from the LORD: 2Stand at the gate of the
house of the LORD and proclaim this message
there: Hear the word of the LORD, all you of
Judah who enter these gates to worship the LORD!
3Thus says the LORD of hosts, the God of Israel:
Reform your ways and your deeds so that I may
dwell with you in this place. 4Do not put your
trust in these deceptive words: "The temple of the
LORD! The temple of the LORD! The temple of
the LORD!" 5Only if you thoroughly reform your
ways and your deeds; if each of you deals justly
with your neighbor; 6if you no longer oppress the
alien, the orphan, and the widow; if you no longer
shed innocent blood in this place or follow after
other gods to your own harm, 7only then will I let
you continue to dwell in this place, in the land I
gave your ancestors long ago and forever.
8But look at you! You put your trust in deceptive
words to your own loss! 9Do you think you can steal
and murder, commit adultery and perjury, sacrifice
to Baal, follow other gods that you do not know,
10and then come and stand in my presence in this
house, which bears my name, and say: "We are safe!
We can commit all these abominations again!"?
11Has this house which bears my name become in
your eyes a den of thieves? I have seen it for my-
self!—oracle of the LORD. 12Go to my place at Shi-
loh, where I made my name dwell in the beginning.
See what I did to it because of the wickedness of my
people Israel. 13And now, because you have com-
mitted all these deeds—oracle of the LORD—be-
cause you did not listen, though I spoke to you
untiringly, and because you did not answer, though
I called you, 14I will do to this house, which bears
my name, in which you trust, and to the place which
I gave you and your ancestors, exactly what I did to
Shiloh. 15I will cast you out of my sight, as I cast
away all your kindred, all the offspring of Ephraim.

This temple sermon of Jeremiah so shocked his contemporaries that they demanded his death (see Jer 26:8, which follows a condensed version of the temple sermon [26:2-6]). Jeremiah had attacked their basic understanding of God's relationship to Israel. He boldly announced that relying on royal covenant theology was useless. The prayer "The temple of the LORD!"—offered continually in God's sanctuary and seen to assure unconditional protection—was a deceit (v. 4). God would not protect Jerusalem. In fact, God would demolish it. Like God's former shrine at Shiloh, which was destroyed by the Philistines (1 Sam 4:1-11), the Jerusalem temple would be laid waste (vv. 12-14).

Jeremiah's offensive message seemed to assert that God, who had made an unconditional promise to David, now intended to break it. If this proved to be true, God would be unreliable, and faith and hope in God would be impossible. In fact, when Jerusalem fell, many Judeans rejected their relationship with God for exactly this reason. They understandably concluded that God had deserted Israel and could not be trusted.

But even as he announced the fall of Jerusalem, Jeremiah insisted that God had remained faithful. God had not abandoned Israel. Rather, Israel had abandoned God. Jeremiah made this claim by pointing to a characteristic of God that royal covenant theology had overlooked: *a God who expects moral action*. Using the traditions of the law given at Sinai, Jeremiah reminded his listeners that the unconditional claims of royal covenant theology were in fact conditioned. In the temple sermon above, verses 5-7 continually repeat the word "if" to express this conditional aspect of the covenant. The absence of moral action was in fact a rejection of the covenant by the people. The fall of Jerusalem occurred not because God was negligent of the relationship but because Israel was. Jeremiah 4:16-18 states this clearly:

Jeremiah 4:16-18

[16]"Make this known to the nations,
announce it against Jerusalem:
Besiegers are coming from the distant land,
shouting their war cry against the cities of Judah."
[17]Like watchers in the fields they surround her,
for she has rebelled against me—oracle of the LORD.
[18]Your conduct, your deeds, have done this to you;
how bitter is this evil of yours,
how it reaches to your very heart!

In his temple sermon (see Jer 7:1-15 above), Jeremiah enumerated some of the deeds and omissions by which Israel rejected the covenant. Verse 9 mentions the failure to follow the Ten Commandments: stealing, murder, adultery, and false worship. Verse 5 cites the lack of justice toward a neighbor. Verse 6 lifts up the unmet expectations of *a God of the marginalized*: failure to respect the alien and care for the orphan and the widow. Jeremiah insisted that such moral failure, not God's negligence of covenant promises, would be the cause of Jerusalem's destruction.

Contemporary Relevance. At a key moment in Israel's history, Jeremiah employed an overlooked characteristic of God (*a God who expects moral action*) to correct a theology that emphasized God's unconditional promises to the detriment of human responsibility. His words remind us that emphasizing some truths of our faith does not assure us that we are doing all that God expects of us. A believer must accept all that God has revealed to live as God requires.

We can rightly feel satisfaction when we worship God regularly and thank God for all we have received. But praise and thanks do not fully express the terms of the covenant God has made with us. Our God also expects moral action, especially toward the vulnerable among us. Nor can our care be limited to only one issue or class of people. Our responsibilities extend to the young and old, to the poor and privileged, to our neighbors and our enemies. We are called to be advocates for child education and prison reform, for the unborn and the environment, for the needs of our families and every family in our world. Jeremiah tells us that living only a part of the covenant is not enough. Adhering to only some of God's expectations is not only incomplete—the fall of Jerusalem testifies that it can also be fatal.

Jeremiah was certain that moral failure had exposed Israel to a destruction that could not be avoided. Prophets frequently used symbolic actions to convey their messages. Jeremiah took a clay flask and smashed it before the elders and priests of the people, saying, "Thus says the LORD of hosts: Thus will I smash this people and this city, as one smashes a clay pot so that it cannot be repaired" (19:11). Exile was inevitable, and Jeremiah demanded that Israel embrace it. To those confined to the besieged city of Jerusalem, he advised surrender to Babylon (21:8-9), and to the exiles already in Babylon, he directed them to accept defeat:

Jeremiah 29:4-7

[4]Thus says the Lord of hosts, the God of Israel, to all the exiles whom I exiled from Jerusalem to Babylon: [5]Build houses and live in them; plant gardens and eat their fruits. [6]Take wives and have sons and daughters; find wives for your sons and give your daughters to husbands, so that they may bear sons and daughters. Increase there; do not decrease. [7]Seek the welfare of the city to which I have exiled you; pray for it to the Lord, for upon its welfare your own depends.

Once Israel had negated its covenant with God, Jeremiah insisted that exile was unavoidable and had to be accepted.

Contemporary Relevance. The prophecy of Jeremiah can offer guidance as we face inevitable losses in our lives. It tells us that there is no benefit in denying what is unescapable. Ultimately, the way forward is to accept what we have lost and continue on. Once a divorce has been finalized, for example, it is of little use to play over and over in our minds what could have or should have been different. The better path is to accept what has happened and open ourselves to a new way of living. When the diagnosis of cancer is indisputable, anger and depression are understandable. But we must ultimately accept our condition and find the courage to take the next constructive step. There will always be failures we must face and losses we cannot escape. Jeremiah shows us that when there is no way around them, it is best to embrace them. Often the only way out is through.

Jeremiah 31:31-34

The New Covenant. [31]See, days are coming—oracle of the LORD—when I will make a new covenant with the house of Israel and the house of Judah. [32]It will not be like the covenant I made with their ancestors the day I took them by the hand to lead them out of the land of Egypt. They broke my covenant, though I was their master—oracle of the LORD. [33]But this is the covenant I will make with the house of Israel after those days—oracle of the LORD. I will place my law within them, and write it upon their hearts; I will be their God, and they shall be my people. [34]They will no longer teach their friends and relatives, "Know the LORD!" Everyone, from least to greatest, shall know me—oracle of the LORD—for I will forgive their iniquity and no longer remember their sin.

Jeremiah: A Prophecy of Building Up

Although Jeremiah was a prophet of doom, he was also a messenger of hope. His mission was both to tear down and to build up. By placing responsibility for the fall of Jerusalem upon the moral failure of the people, Jeremiah protected God from the claim of unfaithfulness. Therefore, faith in God was still possible even in the midst of exile. Hope could be revived once Israel accepted its captivity. Even as Israel suffered through its exile, Jeremiah announced that God was preparing to return the exiles to their land and embrace them again: "With age-old love I have loved you; / so I have kept my mercy toward you. / Again I will build you, and you shall stay built, / virgin Israel; / Carrying your festive tambourines / you shall go forth dancing with merrymakers" (31:3-4).

Jeremiah then announced that a new covenant, a new relationship, would be established between God and God's people:

A new covenant with God was possible. But how was it new? Something can be new when it breaks totally from the past. But new can also indicate an addition to a long-standing arrangement. The new covenant of Jeremiah is of the latter type. Indeed, most of Jeremiah's new covenant is an expression of the prior covenant. Verse 33c states the purpose of the new covenant: "I will be their God, and they shall be my people." This repeats the language of the covenants with Abraham and Moses (Gen 17:7-8; Exod 29:45; Lev 26:45). The God of the new covenant is the same God Israel has always known.

Long-standing characteristics of God are also evident in this new covenant. The new covenant is *freely initiated*. The repeated assertions "I will make" and "I will place" demonstrate that this covenant is grounded in God's free gift (vv. 31b, 33). The *expectation of moral action* guided by the law continues (v. 33b). And the God of the new covenant remains *a God who forgives*. In fact, the relationship can continue only because God is willing to "no longer remember their sin" (v. 34c).

What, then, is new? The newness is found in the human ability to keep the covenant. The previous covenant failed because the people did not keep it (v. 32). So Jeremiah announces that God will find a new way to make the relationship viable: God will not write the law upon stone tablets but upon human hearts (v. 33b). People will no longer need to teach others to know the Lord. Everyone, from the least to the greatest, will know God (v. 34a-b). "Knowing God" does not mean retaining cognitive information about God. It means standing in relationship with God, knowing God as we know a friend or spouse. In other words, "knowing God" is faith: entering into and clinging to a personal relationship with God.

Jeremiah's startling claim is that God will change human hearts so that believers will no longer resist or refuse the relationship God has initiated. This is what makes the covenant new—not God's desire for the relationship but our ability to live it. Because the people were unable to follow the prior covenant, God will establish a new covenant in which God's people will be faithful.

As stunning as this new covenant is, what it promises seems impossible. Living in a relationship with God in which faith is innate, spontaneous, and constant did not become Israel's experience, nor is it ours. To this day both Jews and Christians continue to question God's ways and struggle to believe and to hope. Jeremiah recognized this. That is why he begins the announcement of the new covenant with these words: "See, days are coming" (v. 31a). The change that the new covenant announces will not happen tomorrow. Nor will it happen by human effort. The kind of faith and hope Jeremiah describes will only be possible when God makes us new in a radical way. If we are to believe in the new covenant, we must accept that its actualization belongs to God.

This is a significant "updating" of the terms of faith. We are asked to believe in a God who will change us, who will make us perfectly able to respond. This shift in faith also changes the nature of hope. Hope now directs itself to a future that is completely in God's hands. The object of our hope not only moves into the future but also becomes difficult to visualize. How are we to imagine being able to perfectly fulfill our part of the covenant? We wait in hope for God to act in a way we cannot fully describe.

Contemporary Relevance. As descendants of Abraham we can, of course, continue to hope in what we can describe. We can hope that God will bless us with a loving family and faithful friends. We can hope for the kind of work that not only supports us financially but also provides personal satisfaction and true service to others. We can hope for the strength to overcome obstacles and bear the burdens that every life brings. All such hopes are valid and are true blessings when they are realized.

But the new covenant proposes a larger hope—a hope that is beyond our imagining. It promises a fundamental change in human nature. It thereby reminds us that our future is not exhausted by the hopes we can envision. If the contours of tomorrow were clear, we could direct our hope accordingly. But the hope the new covenant proposes is beyond our imagining and control. The realization of the new covenant lies fully in God's hands. Hope, then, must rest there as well.

This movement of hope actually frees us as people of faith. Although we can and should hope for the things we can anticipate, hope need not be limited to what we can envision. We no longer need to anticipate what God can do for us. Hope itself moves into the arms of faith, clinging more closely to the God who saves and journeys with us. No longer do we need to ask specifically for this blessing or that strength. We can simply trust that God will provide. We can echo the words of Jesus: "[Y]our will be done" (Matt 6:10).

The Return from Babylon: Turning to a New World

In 539 BCE, after defeating the Babylonian army at the battle of Opis, the Persian king Cyrus entered the city of Babylon as its new ruler. The next year (approximately fifty years after the exile began), Cyrus issued a decree allowing the Jewish people to return to their homeland (Ezra 1:2-4). The hope of those who had held fast to their faith in the God of Abraham was realized.

Yet only some of the exiles chose to leave the comforts of Babylon and its new magnanimous ruler. Those who did return faced a grim situation. Jerusalem and the surrounding cities were devastated, and the land was ruined. Some of the people who now inhabited the land did not welcome the returning exiles and frustrated their efforts to rebuild. Although the foundations for a new temple were begun, when those who were old enough to remember the glory of Solomon's temple saw the modest size of the new foundations, they wept (Ezra 3:12). The lack of resources and continuing political interference delayed the temple's construction. As a result, it was not completed until over twenty years after the exiles returned.

The prophets Haggai and Zechariah called for the rebuilding of the temple. Ezra and Nehemiah introduced religious reforms that led to the canonization of the Scriptures and religious practices that still characterize Judaism today. But there would be no return to a political kingdom comparable to the monarchy of David. Judah remained a small territory consisting of the lands immediately surrounding Jerusalem. It was ruled first by the Persians (539–332 BCE) and then by the Greeks (332–175 BCE). A limited freedom under Jewish leadership was achieved under the Maccabees from 175 to 63 BCE. But this self-rule came to an end when the Roman general Pompey annexed the territory of Judah into the Roman Empire.

Although Israel's political fortunes waned, its religious insight grew significantly. Spurred by the prophets of the exile, Israel began to paint its faith on an ever-larger canvas. Because God was creator and ruler of all, God's power was not limited to the existing circumstances of history. The powers of this world and its structures could be overturned by God and made new.

During this period, a new kind of writing began to emerge. Today we call it "apocalyptic" literature, from the Greek word that means "to uncover" or "to reveal." What this literature attempted to reveal was the ultimate will of God for Israel and, indeed, for all humanity. From its beginnings with Abraham, Israel's faith was directed toward the future, carrying the hope of what God would do in human history. Israel's great prophets often referred to "the day of the LORD" to mark a future day when God would act in Israel's life and bring about blessing or judgment (see Isa 2:12; Amos 5:18-20). After the exile, apocalyptic writers began to use "the day of the LORD" to mark the day when God would bring about a new structure to our present existence. Using fantastic imagery, they announced God's ultimate victory over evil and the establishment of a new age. Building upon Jeremiah's claim that a new covenant would re-create human hearts, apocalyptic writers proclaimed that God would also create a new world.

Apocalyptic literature flourished for approximately four hundred years (200 BCE–200 CE) in both Jewish and Christian contexts. Although only two apocalyptic books have been included in our Bibles (Daniel and Revelation), apocalyptic sections can also be found in other biblical writings (e.g., Isa 24–27; Ezek 38–39; Mark 13).

Apocalyptic works share a common worldview: God is never indifferent to the evil present in our world and is committed to establishing a new world order of justice. This order includes bodily resurrection for those who are faithful to God. Apocalyptic thought therefore provided the context in which early Christians were able to understand and accept the resurrection of Jesus.

This apocalyptic worldview affected Israel's faith and hope. Faith became believing in and clinging to a God who is all-powerful and determined to destroy every evil of the world. Hope was trusting that a day would come when God would act, bringing all creation into conformity with God's will. After the exile, both faith and hope turned toward the God of the World to Come.

One place in the Bible where we find this apocalyptic perspective is in the book of Zechariah, which contains the oracles (prophetic messages) of two prophets. Chapters 1–8 record the sayings of a prophet (often called First Zechariah) who was active in the period immediately after the return from exile. Chapters 9–14 contain the oracles of a prophet (Second Zechariah) who was active about 150 years later. This later prophet announces that God will deliver Jerusalem from the power of foreign nations. But his description of the Jerusalem that God will bring about clearly pushes the boundaries of the present world:

Zechariah 14:6-9

Jerusalem Restored. 6On that day there will no
longer be cold or frost. 7There will be one continu-
ous day—it is known to the LORD—not day and
night, for in the evening there will be light. 8On that
day, fresh water will flow from Jerusalem, half to the
eastern sea, and half to the western sea. This will be
so in summer and in winter. 9The LORD will be king
over the whole earth; on that day the LORD will be
the only one, and the LORD's name the only one.

This is not a description of God acting within the parameters of the world as we know it. This is a radical altering of climate, water flow, day, and night.

Like Zechariah, the book of Isaiah also contains oracles from several time periods. A group of passages typically referred to as Third Isaiah (chaps. 56–66) were likely written in the postexilic period and present a vision of a new creation, expanding faith and hope beyond the present world. The following passage from Third Isaiah provides a glimpse of God's ultimate promise:

Isaiah 65:17-20

A World Renewed. 17See, I am creating new
heavens
and a new earth;
The former things shall not be remembered
nor come to mind.
18Instead, shout for joy and be glad forever
in what I am creating.
Indeed, I am creating Jerusalem to be a joy
and its people to be a delight;
19I will rejoice in Jerusalem
and exult in my people.
No longer shall the sound of weeping be
heard there,
or the sound of crying;
20No longer shall there be in it
an infant who lives but a few days,
nor anyone who does not live a full
lifetime;
One who dies at a hundred years shall be
considered a youth,
and one who falls short of a hundred shall
be thought accursed.

The prophet Zechariah (Giacomo Gavedoni)

In this passage, God who is creator creates once again. God who is savior saves in a more profound way. There will be a new earth without weeping or loss (v. 17, 19), where children will not die and where those who live one hundred years will be considered young (v. 20). The prophet clearly sees a world beyond the present one.

Another postexilic passage from Isaiah, located in a section known as the "Little Apocalypse" (chaps. 24–27), dares to push the promise of a future world even further:

Isaiah 25:6-9

6On this mountain the LORD of hosts
will provide for all peoples
A feast of rich food and choice wines,
juicy, rich food and pure, choice wines.
7On this mountain he will destroy
the veil that veils all peoples,
The web that is woven over all nations.
8He will destroy death forever.
The Lord GOD will wipe away
the tears from all faces;
The reproach of his people he will remove
from the whole earth; for the LORD has
spoken.
9On that day it will be said:
"Indeed, this is our God; we looked to him,
and he saved us!
This is the LORD to whom we looked;
let us rejoice and be glad that he has
saved us!"

This passage presents a glorious banquet that will occur on the last day, the Day of the Lord (v. 9). It will be celebrated on the temple mountain in Jerusalem and will include all peoples (vv. 6-7). As in Isaiah 65:17-20, there will be no more crying or pain (v. 8b-c). But here Isaiah pushes the horizons of hope even further. The ultimate evil will no longer have power over humanity: "He will destroy death forever" (v. 8a). Here the faith of Abraham begins to perceive God's final plan for us.

Contemporary Relevance. When we read apocalyptic passages announcing a new creation, we can too easily dismiss them as mere poetry. How can daylight be continuous or human suffering eliminated? How can death come to an end? We can hope for what is reasonable, but can we hope for what is unimaginable? We can hope for progress in the exercise of justice, but when we face the complexities of prejudice and racism in our society, can we hope for a world in which injustice is no more? We can hope that real steps will be taken to curb hatred and violence, but when we see the entrenched conflicts around the world, is it possible to hope for a world at peace?

Religious believers must always guard against wishful thinking. We must acknowledge the reality of evil and the suffocating hold it has upon our world. Apocalyptic writers knew such evil firsthand. Yet their visions of a perfect world are more than fancy or speculation. Their grand visions are meant to remind us that God cannot be limited by what we think is possible. Yes, complete justice and world peace may be beyond our imagining. But we are not the creator of the earth or the savior of the world. Apocalyptic writers continually insist that our vision of God is too small. It is not up to us to say what God can do. God is God, and we are not. We believe in the God who once questioned Abraham: "Is anything too marvelous for the LORD to do?" (Gen 18:14).

Resurrection from the Dead

By the age of 25, Alexander the Great had conquered a vast territory that stretched from Greece south to Egypt and east to India. With his defeat of the Persians, Palestine came under Greek control. When Alexander died in 323 BCE, his empire was divided among his generals. Greek rule promoted Greek culture. In the territory of Judah, this Hellenization process remained relatively peaceful until Antiochus IV came to the throne in 175 BCE. His behavior was eccentric and unstable. He claimed for himself the title *Epiphanes*, which meant "God made manifest." (Playing on this title, his opponents named him *Epimanes*, which meant "out of his mind.")

When Antiochus IV Epiphanes heard that Judea was in revolt over his Hellenizing policies, he attacked Jerusalem and slaughtered its inhabitants. Second Maccabees 5:11-14 states that in the space of three days, forty thousand people were killed and another forty thousand were taken into slavery. Antiochus forbade Jewish practices. Regular temple sacrifices ceased. Circumcision, observance of the Sabbath, and the possession of sacred texts were outlawed. Jews were forced to eat food that was forbidden by the law. In 167 BCE, an altar to the Greek god Zeus was set up in the Jerusalem temple (1 Macc 1:41-64). Any resistance to these policies was punishable by death. Many Jews chose martyrdom.

Antiochus IV died in 164 BCE, only three years after the profanation of the Jerusalem temple. But the shock of his merciless persecution continued to reverberate among faithful Jews. How was it possible to believe in a covenant with God when God permitted the slaughter of so many of the most faithful members of the community? What sense was there in being God's people when God seemed indifferent to their survival? The violent persecution by Antiochus understandably caused many Jews to abandon faith in the God of Abraham. Like the exiles who assimilated into Babylonian culture, many Jews in the time of Antiochus experienced overwhelming pressure to abandon their faith and culture and live as Greeks. But again, as in the exile, some were able to cling tightly to faith and hope in the God of Israel.

During this difficult period, and in light of the persecution of Antiochus, some Jews came to believe in the resurrection of the dead. Drawing upon the apocalyptic vision that was already on the rise, they came to believe that on the last day, when God was expected to bring about a new world, those who had been slayed by Antiochus would be raised from death. God was faithful because God—a God of the World to Come—would be faithful in the end.

This belief in resurrection emerged late in our faith tradition. There are very few passages in the Old Testament that explicitly refer to the resurrection of individuals. One of them is found in the apocalyptic book of Daniel:

Daniel 12:1-3

The Resurrection.

1"At that time there shall arise Michael,
the great prince,
guardian of your people;
It shall be a time unsurpassed in distress
since the nation began until that time.
At that time your people shall escape,
everyone who is found written in the book.
2Many of those who sleep
in the dust of the earth shall awake;
Some to everlasting life,
others to reproach and everlasting
disgrace.
3But those with insight shall shine brightly
like the splendor of the firmament,
And those who lead the many to justice
shall be like the stars forever.

This passage presents an apocalyptic vision of the last day, when the angel Michael will execute God's justice. Verse 2 affirms that on that day the dead will be raised up. It is important to understand clearly what this passage proclaims. God is not said to raise up the dead into a spiritual existence. God intends to return them to life *in bodily form*. According to New Testament scholar N. T. Wright, when verse 3 compares those who are raised to stars, it indicates that those who are raised will be part of the material world. Their state, however, will not be exactly as it was before death. They will shine brightly in a glorified form as rulers of a new creation. (See Wright, *The Resurrection of the Son of God* [Fortress Press, 2003], 109–15.)

Another passage confirming Jewish faith in the resurrection of the dead can be found in 2 Maccabees 7, a graphic account of the torture of a mother and her seven sons, all of whom refused to eat pork in violation of Jewish law. Explicit confirmation of bodily resurrection is found in the words of one of the sons, who willingly stretches out his hands for amputation, saying: "It was from Heaven that I received these [hands]; for the sake of his laws I disregard them; from him I hope to receive them again" (2 Macc 7:11). The young man clearly believes that the just will receive their bodies back on the last day.

In the ancient world, only Jews believed in bodily resurrection. Although a bold and unprecedented claim, it was a logical development in a tradition that understood God as a savior and creator. God's saving power was extended beyond the grave, and the God who created the material world was now seen to promise a material afterlife. God had made creation good (Gen 1:31). Therefore, the material world would be a part of God's ultimate plan.

As the Jewish faith tradition accepted Isaiah's assertion that death would be no more (25:8), it dared to believe that the just would be raised up in bodily form to enter a new heaven and a new earth. Faith and hope in the God of the Nations had become faith and hope in the God of the World to Come.

The Resurrection of the Body

Throughout most of the Hebrew Bible, death is seen as final. No place of joy is envisioned after this life. The place of the dead (usually called *Sheol*) is a place of stillness, darkness, and complete helplessness (Ps 6:6; 16:10; Isa 5:14; 38:18). After the exile, and influenced by the martyrdoms under Antiochus IV, some Jews began to believe that God would raise up the just, re-creating them, body and spirit, on the last day.

Not all Jews accepted bodily resurrection. Judaism after the exile was a vibrant and diverse reality with many distinct groups advocating various theological positions. Bodily resurrection was championed by the Pharisees. Jesus sided with them against the Sadducees, who did not accept it (Mark 12:18).

Even today, many Christians do not embrace the importance of bodily resurrection, focusing only on our spiritual union with God after death. But the Apostles' Creed clearly asserts that we believe in "the resurrection of the body."

At Jesus' return on the last day, both the living and the dead will be raised up in bodily form to participate in the new creation. Christians have seen this as the goal of our covenant with God from the beginning. As Paul taught: "If the Spirit of the one who raised Jesus from the dead dwells in you, the one who raised Christ from the dead will give life to your mortal bodies also" (Rom 8:11).

In its explanation of the Apostles' Creed, the *Catechism of the Catholic Church* states: "By death the soul is separated from the body, but in the resurrection God will give incorruptible life to our body, transformed by reunion with our soul. Just as Christ is risen and lives for ever, so all of us will rise at the last day" (1016).

EXPLORING LESSON THREE

1. a) Why did the Babylonian exile cause a crisis of faith and hope for the Israelite people?

b) Have you experienced a time when it felt like God had abandoned you? If so, how did you come through that time with your faith and hope intact?

2. What is "royal covenant theology," and how did Jeremiah understand it?

3. According to Jeremiah's temple sermon, how did the people fail in their covenant relationship with God (Jer 7:1-15)?

4. How would you explain Jeremiah's "new covenant" in your own words (Jer 31:31-34)?

5. How does the nature of faith and hope change after Jeremiah's prophecy of a new covenant with God?

6. a) What is apocalyptic literature, and in what circumstances did it emerge?

   b) How do faith and hope evolve with the emergence of an apocalyptic worldview?

7. After reading the apocalyptic passages in Zechariah (14:6-9) and Isaiah (65:17-20; 25:6-9), which apocalyptic image or expectation resonates with you the most and why?

8. How was belief in the resurrection of the dead a natural development in the faith and hope of Israel?

9. As Christians, we have inherited faith and hope in the resurrection of the dead from the Jewish faith tradition. Does it surprise you to learn that we believe in a *bodily* resurrection? Do you find this a challenging or a comforting belief? In what way?

10. What insight about faith or hope can you share with your group after studying and reflecting on the prophetic texts explored in this lesson?

CLOSING PRAYER

Prayer

See, I am creating new heavens
and a new earth;
The former things shall not be remembered
nor come to mind. (Isa 65:17)

God of faith and hope, our faith in you gives us great hope for the future, when all your promises will be fulfilled, and nothing will separate us from you. Help us live in joyful expectation now, and increase our faith in the plans you have for all your people. Today we pray for those most in need of your promises, especially . . .

LESSON FOUR

Faith and Hope in the Gospel

Begin your personal study and group discussion with a simple and sincere prayer such as:

Prayer

Lord God, help us listen with the ears of our hearts as we spend time with your word. Reveal yourself to us today as you have revealed yourself through the ages, and strengthen in us your gifts of faith, hope, and love.

Read pages 58–67, Lesson Four.

Respond to the questions on pages 68–70, Exploring Lesson Four.

The Closing Prayer on page 70 is for your personal use and may be used at the end of group discussion.

FAITH AND HOPE IN THE GOSPEL

In the first three lessons of this study, we have seen how faith, which began with Abraham, developed into a conviction that God would bring about a new world. In this lesson, we will examine how Jesus inherits and continues this Jewish faith tradition.

The lesson will be divided into three sections. The first presents Jesus as a herald of God's coming kingdom. Jesus had faith that God would act to destroy the evil and injustice of our present world. His hope was that God would act soon. He proclaimed that in God's kingdom, the most vulnerable members of society hold a special place. The second section explores how Jesus' apocalyptic emphasis on the coming kingdom did not preclude him from believing that God also cares for our present needs. We will consider how Jesus encouraged faith through miracles, taught that faith is a gift, and warned against the opposite of faith, which is worry. In a third section, we will examine how faith and hope are changed by Jesus' death and resurrection. Jesus, who announced the coming kingdom, became, in fact, the center of the gospel. Our faith and hope now depend on the proclamation that he is risen.

Jesus' Gospel: The Future Kingdom

Jesus believed and hoped in the God of the World to Come. As a Jew of his time, he believed in the God of the Family and understood that the God of the Nations had made an irrevocable promise to David. But Jesus also had faith that God, as savior, could destroy the injustice of the present world and, as creator, could bring about a new one. Jesus had hope that God would bring about the new order of God's kingdom soon.

Jesus' faith and hope were the basis upon which he announced his "gospel," or "good news." The gospel he proclaimed was that God's kingdom was near and that God would destroy the evil that is part of our present world and make all things new.

The three Synoptic Gospels are united in their assertion that Jesus' mission was to announce this good news of the coming kingdom of God. Mark states, "Jesus came to Galilee proclaiming the gospel of God: 'This is the time of fulfillment. The kingdom of God is at hand. Repent, and believe in the gospel'" (1:14-15). This same proclamation is affirmed by Matthew (3:2; 4:23) and Luke (4:43; 8:1; 11:20; 17:21).

Consistent with Jewish belief concerning the Day of the Lord, Jesus believed that the coming kingdom would be a time when evil would be destroyed. This is attested in his explanation of the parable of the Weeds:

> *Matthew 13:41-43*
>
> 41The Son of Man will send his angels, and they will collect out of his kingdom all who cause others to sin and all evildoers. 42They will throw them into the fiery furnace, where there will be wailing and grinding of teeth. 43Then the righteous will shine like the sun in the kingdom of their Father. Whoever has ears ought to hear.

Jesus Prays for the Kingdom

A particularly clear expression of Jesus' faith and hope in the future kingdom of God is found in the Lord's Prayer. There are two versions of this prayer that have come down to us: Matthew 6:9-13 and Luke 11:2-4. The importance of this prayer cannot be overstated. The prayer derives from Jesus himself, and it crystallizes what Jesus saw as the most important request to make to God: the coming of God's kingdom. Here is Matthew's version:

> *Matthew 6:9-13*
>
> **The Lord's Prayer.**
> 9"This is how you are to pray:
>
> Our Father in heaven,
> hallowed be your name,
> 10your kingdom come,
> your will be done,
> on earth as in heaven.
> 11Give us today our daily bread;
> 12and forgive us our debts,
> as we forgive our debtors;
> 13and do not subject us to the final test,
> but deliver us from the evil one.

After an address to God as Father, the Lord's Prayer makes six petitions to God (vv. 9c, 10a, 10b, 11, 12, 13). Most of them relate to the coming of God's kingdom. This is stated most clearly in verse 10a: "[Y]our kingdom come." But this same request is repeated throughout the prayer in various ways:

- Verse 10b asks for the coming of the kingdom by praying that God's will, already perfectly followed in heaven, will be done on earth. This is a plea for the day when God's rule will extend everywhere.
- Verse 9c also refers to the coming kingdom. The Greek verb used in this verse is in a tense that indicates a one-time action. Therefore, this petition asks that God's name be hallowed or glorified at a particular time. That time is the Day of the Lord, when God's kingdom will be fully established.
- Verse 12 asks God to forgive us our "debts" (our sins or "trespasses"). But again, the tense of the verb indicates one-time action. Therefore, the petition is not for daily forgiveness but for forgiveness on the day when it will be most important: the day of final judgment.
- Verse 13 seeks protection on the last day. It asks to be spared a negative judgment at "the final test" and delivered from the power of "the evil one" (Satan), who will be defeated when the kingdom arrives.

Although the Lord's Prayer is oriented toward God's future kingdom, one verse seems to address a present need: **"Give us today our daily bread"** (Matt 6:11). According to scholars, the Greek word translated as "daily" can carry either an immediate sense ("our *present* bread"—referring to the bread we need now), or it can point to the future ("our *coming* bread"—referring to the bread we will share in God's kingdom).

The Lord's Prayer is not about Jesus. It is a prayer *of* Jesus to the God of Israel. The One addressed as Father is the God revealed in the Jewish tradition—the God who *listens, saves us* from evil, and has the power to *create* the world to come. This prayer asks that the One who *freely initiated* a relationship with humanity will now freely initiate a new world.

Contemporary Relevance. Every Christian knows the Lord's Prayer. Many of us were taught it as the first formal way to speak to God. We learned the words of this prayer long before we knew what "hallowed" or "trespass" meant. We continue to pray it at every Eucharist, whenever we pray the rosary, and as part of our personal prayers. But how often do we stop to reflect on what the words of the prayer really mean?

We have discussed how the petitions of this prayer ask for the coming of God's future kingdom. Yet it is likely that, for most of our lives, we have understood it as asking for God's assistance in our present lives rather than pleading for a world to come. We typically understand the prayer as asking to hallow God's name today, to forgive someone who has offended us in our present circumstances, and to protect us from evil influences now.

There is certainly nothing wrong with praying the Lord's Prayer in this way. Asking God for our present needs is valid and appropriate. Yet if we appreciate the future apocalyptic sense in which Jesus first offered this prayer, it can broaden the way in which we pray it. When we recognize that praying for the coming of God's kingdom is asking God to save not only us but also all creation, this prayer widens to include the entire world. When we understand that God's will is to destroy every evil, then the Lord's Prayer expands into an appeal for the end of war, greed, prejudice, and every injustice.

Because God's kingdom has not yet been fully realized in our world, the Lord's Prayer remains our prayer. Each day as we pray it, we can ask in faith and hope that every evil we can imagine—personal or global, present or future—be destroyed. We may be dismayed at how much is wrong in our world and frustrated by how little power we have to change it. By praying Jesus' prayer to the Father, we can ask God to act, to re-create our world, and to bring about the day when God's power will reign on earth as it does now in heaven.

Jesus and the God of the Marginalized

As Jesus proclaimed the gospel of the coming kingdom of God, he directed his concern in a special way to those who were considered unimportant or powerless by the world's standards, those on the margins of society. Jesus' attention to the poor and powerless was no innovation on his part but was a continuation of the Jewish tradition. As a Jew of his time, Jesus had faith in the God who had been consistently revealed as the *God of the marginalized*. In the call of the refugee Abraham, God was first revealed as a God of the powerless and the homeless. Even when Israel was at the height of its political power, the test for its faithfulness to God was its care for the poor. The Mosaic law consistently directed attention to the widow, the orphan, and the stranger. Jesus took up this emphasis. His ministry was to the subsistence farmers and the fishermen of Galilee; to outcasts, prostitutes, and tax collectors; to those experiencing illness and disability. He announced good news to the poor (Matt 11:5; Luke 4:18).

Not only did Jesus preach to the poor, but he was poor himself. At his birth Jesus was not laid in a royal bed but in a feeding trough for animals (Luke 2:7). Although Mary's husband, Joseph, is identified as a carpenter or builder (Matt 13:55), Jesus did not ultimately adopt this trade as a means of income. He was an itinerant preacher who was dependent upon the support of others (Luke 8:1-3) and who lived without a home (Matt 8:20). Jesus was crucified as a lowly criminal, experiencing a death that Paul describes as the death of a slave (Phil 2:7-8). Jesus therefore proclaimed the coming kingdom of God as a marginalized member of society. Faith for Jesus was faith in the God of the vulnerable. His hope and expectation was that, with the coming of God's kingdom, those who were without power or resources would be blessed.

This hope is crystallized in the beatitudes of Jesus, which are widely considered the heart of his gospel. The beatitudes, which appear in two Gospel passages (Matt 5:3-12; Luke 6:20-23), succinctly connect the marginalized to the coming kingdom of God. We will examine Luke's version:

Luke 6:20-23

20 And raising his eyes toward his disciples he said:
"Blessed are you who are poor,
for the kingdom of God is yours.
21 Blessed are you who are now hungry,
for you will be satisfied.
Blessed are you who are now weeping,
for you will laugh.
22 Blessed are you when people hate you,
and when they exclude and insult you,

and denounce your name as evil
on account of the Son of Man.
23Rejoice and leap for joy on that day!
Behold, your reward
will be great in heaven.
For their ancestors treated the prophets
in the same way.

To appreciate the importance of the beatitudes, it is helpful to understand that the Greek word our texts translate as "blessed" (*makarios*) means "fortunate," "prosperous," or "free from care." "Blessed" certainly carries this sense, but "happy" hits closer to the mark. In the beatitudes, Jesus is identifying those who should be considered happy, successful, or well-off. He identifies these "happy ones" as the poor, hungry, weeping, hated, and excluded.

In what sense are such people happy? Jesus is not suggesting some silver lining to poverty or hunger. He is not asking us to see a secret goodness in being hated or excluded. Rather, Jesus is telling the disfavored members of society that God's kingdom is coming. He is announcing that God's kingdom *belongs* to them (v. 20). When it arrives, their destitute condition will be reversed. Then they will be satisfied and laugh (v. 21). They will "[r]ejoice and leap for joy *on that day*" (v. 23, emphasis added). Those who are not happy now will be happy then.

The perspective of the beatitudes extends throughout the Gospels. The fortunes of those who are lowly or rejected are consistently reversed. Mary, Jesus' mother, glorifies the God who lifts up the lowly and fills the hungry with good things (Luke 1:52-53). A wayward and impoverished son is embraced and dressed in the finest robe (Luke 15:22). A poor beggar is welcomed to the great patriarch Abraham's side (Luke 16:22). A woman caught in adultery is treated with dignity (John 8:11). Jesus is the guest of a despised tax collector (Luke 19:5). A condemned criminal enters paradise (Luke 23:43).

We have seen how the prophet Isaiah envisioned God's kingdom as a great feast (25:6-9). Jesus uses this image in his parable of the Great Feast to tell us that the first to enter the feast of the kingdom are "the poor and the crippled, the blind and the lame" (Luke 14:21b). The marginalized and vulnerable, then, have the first claim on the kingdom of God. In a tense exchange, Jesus tells the respected chief priests and elders of the people: "Amen, I say to you, tax collectors and prostitutes are entering the kingdom of God before you" (Matt 21:31b). Time and again, the Gospels insist that the coming kingdom belongs to those of inferior status.

Jesus' interactions with children can also be understood as encounters with the marginalized. Parents of Jesus' day, like all parents, loved their children. But in the ancient world, until children reached the age of maturity, they had no legal status and were seen to lack full personhood. In his teaching, Jesus uses the humble status of children to announce the central role of the marginalized in the coming kingdom:

Luke 9:46-48

The Greatest in the Kingdom. 46An argument arose among the disciples about which of them was the greatest. 47Jesus realized the intention of their hearts and took a child and placed it by his side 48and said to them, "Whoever receives this child in my name receives me, and whoever receives me receives the one who sent me. For the one who is least among all of you is the one who is the greatest."

The child in this scene embodies Jesus' gospel. The least among us (in this case, a child) is the greatest. Those who receive such lowly members of society receive Jesus, the God who sent him, and God's kingdom.

The marginalized status of children is also foundational to understanding why Jesus blesses them:

Mark 10:13-16

Blessing of the Children. [13]And people were bringing children to him that he might touch them, but the disciples rebuked them. [14]When Jesus saw this he became indignant and said to them, "Let the children come to me; do not prevent them, for the kingdom of God belongs to such as these. [15]Amen, I say to you, whoever does not accept the kingdom of God like a child will not enter it." [16]Then he embraced them and blessed them, placing his hands on them.

Artistic representations of this scene can be found in Christian nurseries throughout the world. But this passage is more than an attractive affirmation of Jesus' love for children. Although childlike qualities of openness and innocence certainly characterize God's reign, the primary purpose of children in this scene is to represent the powerless and insignificant. This explains why the disciples try to keep the children away (v. 13): Children were not deemed worthy of Jesus' time. When Jesus receives and blesses them, it is another example of God's favor to "the least among us." Jesus' words here echo the beatitude "Blessed are you who are poor, / for the kingdom of God is yours" (Luke 6:20).

Jesus' gospel message concerning the marginalized reaches a high point in the account of the Judgment of the Nations, found only in Matthew's Gospel:

Matthew 25:31-40

The Judgment of the Nations. [31]"When the Son of Man comes in his glory, and all the angels with him, he will sit upon his glorious throne, [32]and all the nations will be assembled before him. And he will separate them one from another, as a shepherd separates the sheep from the goats. [33]He will place the sheep on his right and the goats on his left. [34]Then the king will say to those on his right, 'Come, you who are blessed by my Father. Inherit the kingdom prepared for you from the foundation of the world. [35]For I was hungry and you gave me food, I was thirsty and you gave me drink, a stranger and you welcomed me, [36]naked and you clothed me, ill and you cared for me, in prison and you visited me.' [37]Then the righteous will answer him and say, 'Lord, when did we see you hungry and feed you, or thirsty and give you drink? [38]When did we see you a stranger and welcome you, or naked and clothe you? [39]When did we see you ill or in prison, and visit you?' [40]And the king will say to them in reply, 'Amen, I say to you, whatever you did for one of these least brothers of mine, you did for me.'

This passage visualizes the coming kingdom of God, depicting the moment when Jesus, the Son of Man, decides who will enter the kingdom. Jesus divides those before him into two groups: the just (or the "righteous"; v. 37) who are worthy of the kingdom, and the unjust who are not. (Jesus' words to the just are quoted above. In the remainder of the passage, Jesus addresses the unjust, promising a very different outcome [25:41-46].)

This famous Last Judgment scene is in continuity with Jesus' ministry to the marginalized. Jesus' gospel proclamation is that the kingdom belongs to them. This scene reveals that to enter the kingdom one must serve the hungry, the thirsty, the naked, the stranger, the imprisoned, and the sick. The Lord of the Last Judgment is the poor man from Nazareth. He stands with the vulnerable and the marginalized. What we do for them, we do for him (v. 40).

Contemporary Relevance. The identification of the Son of Man with the most vulnerable among us forces us to reconsider what often passes as Christian charity. No one will deny that following Jesus involves sharing what we have with those who have less. All too often, however, such actions can become self-congratulatory exercises. As we give from our largesse, we feel satisfaction that we have made the lives of others less burdensome. This is noble, to be sure. But it is not the gospel. We are not called to serve our brothers and sisters in need simply to help them. We serve them because they own the kingdom (Luke 6:20). With and through them, everyone will enter God's reign. Our biblical tradition consistently recognizes the most vulnerable among us as recipients of God's special care. It is by identifying with these brothers and sisters of Christ that we gain access to the world to come (Matt 25:34, 40).

Jesus' Gospel: The Present Journey

Although the heart of Jesus' gospel was the future kingdom of God, he did not ignore God's saving action in our present lives. As a faithful Jew, Jesus understood that from the time God first spoke to Abraham, God was revealed as *a God of the journey* who accompanies and provides for those who have faith. Therefore, Jesus' faith was not only in a God who would bring about a new creation but also in a God who helps believers in their present circumstances.

Faith and Jesus' Healing Miracles

In the Gospels, this faith in God's saving presence is closely associated with Jesus' healing miracles. Jesus connects his healing power with faith when he cures a woman with a hemorrhage ("Daughter, your faith has saved you"; Mark 5:34), a man with leprosy ("Stand up and go; your faith has saved you"; Luke 17:19), and a man who is blind ("Go your way; your faith has saved you"; Mark 10:52). A centurion's faith accompanies Jesus' healing of the man's servant (Luke 7:9), and a Canaanite woman's faith is the occasion for Jesus to drive out a demon (Matt 15:28). A man who is paralyzed is healed when Jesus sees the faith of the friends who carry him (Mark 2:5).

In Mark 5:21-43, Jairus, a synagogue official, asks Jesus to heal his daughter, who is at home. Jesus begins to walk with him to his house. On the way, news arrives that the young girl has died. Jesus says to Jairus, "Do not be afraid; just have faith" (5:36). They continue walking. After entering the official's house, Jesus brings the girl back to life (5:42). Here, literally in the context of a journey, faith is shown as trust that God will provide what is vital for human life.

The faith Jesus associates with his deeds of power is faith in the God who journeys with us and can free us from sickness and evil in our present circumstances. This faith, however, is not divorced from faith in God's coming kingdom. In fact, the most compelling purpose for Jesus' miracles is that they indicate the promise and inbreaking of God's reign. Jesus does not heal only to alleviate present suffering. His miracles are signs that God's kingdom is at hand. As Jesus says to his opponents, "[I]f it is by the finger of God that [I] drive out demons, then the kingdom of God has come upon you" (Luke 11:20). Faith in Jesus' power to heal in the present is faith in the God who will bring about a new creation in the future.

The Corporal Works of Mercy

The corporal works of mercy are charitable actions by which we come to the aid of a neighbor who is in bodily need (see *Catechism of the Catholic Church* 2447). These works derive from the words of Jesus in Matthew 25:35-36. Jesus mentions six actions (feeding the hungry, sheltering the homeless, clothing the naked, visiting the sick and imprisoned), and the church has added a seventh: burying the dead. This is a reminder that the six actions mentioned by Jesus do not exhaust the ways we can show mercy to others.

Pope Francis has followed this tradition by suggesting an eighth corporal work of mercy: care for our common home. This work requires "simple daily gestures which break with the logic of violence, exploitation and selfishness" that denigrate the natural environment of our created world (Pope Francis, Message on the World Day of Prayer for the Care of Creation, September 9, 2016).

Faith as God's Gift

Because Jesus believes that God journeys with believers, he calls those who follow him to have faith that God will provide for them today. Yet the faith Jesus seeks does not flow from a human source. Faith always remains God's gift. This aspect of faith is illustrated in an important saying of Jesus', made in reply to the disciples' request that Jesus increase their faith: "If you have faith the size of a mustard seed, you would say to [this] mulberry tree, 'Be uprooted and planted in the sea,' and it would obey you" (Luke 17:6; see also Matt 17:20).

This passage does not provide a strategy for relocating mulberry trees (or, in Matthew's version, mountains). It uses hyperbole to stress the extreme imbalance between God's power and our faith. When God brings about goodness in our world, we are expected to cooperate through faith. But God's action dwarfs anything we can contribute. It is the difference between a mountain and a mustard seed. The disciples are right to ask for an increase in faith because whatever faith they express flows from God's generosity.

Contemporary Relevance. One of the blessings of being a pastor is encountering amazing faith in those to whom you minister. I will always remember a woman from my parish who was 30 years old and diagnosed with an aggressive and deadly form of cancer. For ten months, I visited her as she endured one invasive procedure after another. In each of those visits, she expressed her faith that God was with her and would never forget her. When I spoke to her for the last time, just a few days before her death, I admitted that if our circumstances had been reversed, I doubted that I could have found such faith as hers. She smiled at me and said, "When I was first diagnosed, I panicked. I said to myself, 'I will never be strong enough to deal with this.' But, Father, here is what I have learned: If you can pull together even two percent of the faith you need, God will provide the rest."

When Jesus compares our faith to the size of a mustard seed, he indicates that even a little faith will be enough. When we must face a crisis in our family—a marriage coming apart at the seams, a child or a grandchild who has lost their way—Jesus asks us to pull together a small amount of faith and assures us it will make a difference. When someone we have loved dies, when we realize that if we live long enough, our health will fail and we will become dependent on others, Jesus says, "Gather together whatever faith you can find and give it to me. We will face the future together."

Faith in the Gospel of John

Because John's Gospel professes that God's eternal Word has become flesh in Jesus (1:1-18), faith for John is not simply believing in God, but believing *in Jesus* as the revealer and embodiment of God. The very purpose of John's Gospel is to bring about such faith. It is written "that you may [come to] believe that Jesus is the Messiah, the Son of God" (20:31).

Faith as the Opposite of Worry

Jesus also speaks of faith by warning us about its opposite: worry. When we do not place our faith in a God who journeys with us, our lives soon fill with unrest and anxiety. Jesus addresses our tendency to worry in a famous passage found both in Matthew (6:25-33) and Luke (12:22-31). Here is Luke's version:

Luke 12:22-31

Dependence on God. 22He said to [his] disciples, "Therefore I tell you, do not worry about your life and what you will eat, or about your body and what you will wear. 23For life is more than food and the body more than clothing. 24Notice the ravens: they do not sow or reap; they have neither storehouse nor barn, yet God feeds them. How much more important are you than birds! 25Can any of you by worrying add a moment to your life-span? 26If even the smallest things are

> beyond your control, why are you anxious about the rest? 27Notice how the flowers grow. They do not toil or spin. But I tell you, not even Solomon in all his splendor was dressed like one of them. 28If God so clothes the grass in the field that grows today and is thrown into the oven tomorrow, will he not much more provide for you, O you of little faith? 29As for you, do not seek what you are to eat and what you are to drink, and do not worry anymore. 30All the nations of the world seek for these things, and your Father knows that you need them. 31Instead, seek his kingdom, and these other things will be given you besides.

In this passage, worry is the antithesis of faith. Jesus asserts that worry can be overcome if we believe in a God who journeys with us and provides for us (vv. 28-29). The power of this passage comes from the union of the *God of the journey* with the *God who creates*. God rules all creation, providing food for the birds of the air (v. 24) and beauty for the flowers of the field (v. 27). This same God will also care for us. Jesus' message is not a negative ("Stop worrying") but a positive ("Have faith in the God who has made all things and will care for you").

This passage addresses our daily needs such as food and clothing. Yet it does not ignore God's great promise of the world to come. It calls us first to believe in God's coming kingdom and then assures us that if we place our faith in the God who makes such a promise, our ordinary needs will be met as well (v. 31).

Contemporary Relevance. These well-known words of Jesus can provide us with three practical strategies for overcoming worry with faith.

1) *Remember who you are.* When anxiety rules our lives, it can reduce us to helplessness. We can be pushed down by fear and begin to question our inherent value. In this passage, Jesus emphasizes our high place in creation. He knows the Scriptures affirm that humans are created in God's image (Gen 1:27), making us little less than heavenly beings (Ps 8:6). By comparing us to birds and flowers, Jesus stresses our high status. When worry tempts us, Jesus calls us to remember our exalted value. We are the very image of God in our world. Jesus calls us to accept our true identity when he remarks, "How much more important are you than birds!" (v. 24).

2) *Worry does not work.* Although this passage insists that faith drives worry out, it also reminds us that worry accomplishes nothing: "Can any of you by worrying add a moment to your life-span?" (v. 25). An alternate translation of this verse is "Can any of you by worrying add inches to your stature?" Worrying is an interior disposition. It cannot add length to our life or height to our appearance. As much as worry can consume us, it makes no impact on the problems we face. Stuck in traffic, worrying will not help us reach our destination sooner. Afraid of failure, worrying will not ensure success. A plan of action or a new approach might change the future. But worry only distracts us from living.

3) *Laughter can help.* In the midst of this passage is a line that is best read with humor: "If even the smallest things are beyond your control, why are you anxious about the rest?" (v. 26). How many times a day do we make small mistakes that trip us up, omissions that send us in the wrong direction, or quick decisions that we regret? We place water on the stove to cook pasta, and fifteen minutes later we realize we forgot to turn on the burner. We come home from dinner at our favorite restaurant and discover we left our credit card on the restaurant table. We throw our paycheck out with the trash.

These mishaps can usually be corrected with a little time and effort, but they remind us how limited our influence over life is. In such moments, we can either become angry at our failure or laugh at our ineptitude. Laughter is the better choice. Such oversights provide an opportunity to remember our limitations and dispel our pride. In this passage, Jesus uses our small mistakes to emphasize how much we must depend on God. If we cannot manage all the small tasks of daily living, why should we worry about large issues over which we have no control? So the next time we send an email without the attachment or leave the house without our phone, it may be best to laugh and pray. The God who journeys with us is more than willing to accept an honest, humble prayer: "Lord, I am grateful that you are guiding the big issues of my life, because I am caught up here looking for my car keys."

Hebrews 11 is another well-known New Testament passage about faith. It catalogs heroes and heroines of Israel who are models of faith, referring to them as a great "cloud of witnesses." The author then names Jesus as the model *par excellence*, the "leader and perfecter of faith" (12:1-2). Who are your models of faith, your own "cloud of witnesses"?

Jesus as Gospel

Throughout his ministry, Jesus announced the coming kingdom of God. Consistently standing within the covenant that God first initiated with Abraham, Jesus professed faith in the God of the World to Come and hope that this new world would soon arrive.

This understanding of faith and hope was altered when Jesus was raised from the dead—not as a spirit but as a real, glorified body (Luke 24:37-43; John 20:27). His disciples, fully aware that the bodily resurrection of the dead was to accompany the end times, saw in Jesus' resurrection the beginning of God's re-creation of the world. They began to announce the good news that God had initiated the kingdom *through Jesus' death and resurrection*. In effect, when Jesus was raised from the dead, he became the heart of the gospel. Accepting him as the risen Lord was accepting God's good news.

Through Jesus' resurrection, the early church began to see a new configuration to God's plan for the world to come. God raised Jesus first, as the inauguration of the kingdom, making him the means through which all the just would be raised. Paul describes this unexpected role of Jesus as "the firstfruits of those who have fallen asleep" (1 Cor 15:20). The agricultural term "firstfruits" refers to the first part of the harvest to be collected. It intrinsically ties Jesus' resurrection (the firstfruits) to the resurrection of the dead that will follow (the full harvest). In God's plan, the resurrection of all the just will take place through one man. All the dead will be brought to life in Christ (1 Cor 15:21-22).

Jesus' resurrection, therefore, was the beginning of our resurrection. It was also the inauguration of God's kingdom. The world to come, the world the apocalyptic writers proclaimed and Jesus announced, had begun. This was good news indeed! The first apostles began to announce that God had initiated the kingdom through Jesus' death and resurrection. Jesus, who had announced the good news of the coming kingdom, now became the very content of that good news: God had begun to destroy the evil of the world, resurrect the just, and bring about a new world through him.

Paul passionately proclaims this gospel in his letters, but we know that some in his communities did not understand or accept it. In Paul's First Letter to the Corinthians, for example, it is clear that the Corinthian believers were content to see their faith as an inner spiritual enlightenment, where bodily resurrection of the dead was not important or expected. But Paul rebukes them in the strongest terms:

1 Corinthians 15:12-19

12But if Christ is preached as raised from the
dead, how can some among you say there is no
resurrection of the dead? 13If there is no resurrec-
tion of the dead, then neither has Christ been
raised. 14And if Christ has not been raised, then
empty [too] is our preaching; empty, too, your
faith. 15Then we are also false witnesses to God,
because we testified against God that he raised

> Christ, whom he did not raise if in fact the dead are not raised. 16For if the dead are not raised, neither has Christ been raised, 17and if Christ has not been raised, your faith is vain; you are still in your sins. 18Then those who have fallen asleep in Christ have perished. 19If for this life only we have hoped in Christ, we are the most pitiable people of all.

Notice how closely Paul ties Christ's resurrection to the resurrection of all the dead. He insists that we cannot have one without the other (vv. 13, 16) and that if we separate them, our faith is empty and in vain (vv. 14, 17). Faith is believing that Christ's resurrection leads to our resurrection. The same is true for hope. Verse 19 insists that if we only have hope for our present life (not for the world to come), we are the most pitiable of people.

Throughout his letters, Paul maintains this cosmic approach to faith and hope. Proclaiming Jesus' resurrection as the inauguration of God's ultimate plan for the world, Paul anticipates a new creation (Gal 6:15). When Paul speaks of "faith in Christ," he is speaking of the whole plan of God with Jesus as its center (Phil 3:9; Gal 2:16). This is his gospel. "[F]aith in Jesus Christ" is not so much faith in *who Jesus is* but faith in *what God has done through him.* "[F]aith in Jesus Christ" is shorthand for faith that God has begun to establish the kingdom through Jesus.

Christ's resurrection changed the contours of faith and hope. Believing was no longer simply embracing the God who would bring about a new world. It was having faith that God had in fact initiated a new world through Jesus. Hope became more than trusting that the new creation would arrive. The ultimate hope for the early church was that the kingdom, which was inaugurated in Jesus' resurrection, would come to completion or fulfillment when Jesus returned in glory. Then, every evil would be destroyed. Then, the promise of Isaiah that God "will destroy death forever" would be realized (Isa 25:8; 1 Cor 15:26). When Jesus returned, the will of God would reign on earth as it does in heaven.

Such faith remains the faith of Christians to this day. When we say that we believe in Jesus, we are confessing that he is Son of God and Lord, but we are also proclaiming that he is the good news: The kingdom of God has begun in his death and resurrection.

Hope follows accordingly. Although Christians hope for many things, the primary hope of the gospel is for Jesus to return and fully establish God's reign. Even as we continue to have faith in a God who listens to us and journeys with us, Christian hope remains directed to the world to come, to that day when the dead will be raised and God will be "all in all" (1 Cor 15:28).

In the first four lessons of this study, we have traced the development of our relationship with God since it first began with Abraham. We have seen how faith and hope have evolved with that relationship, expanding from the simple conviction that God will care for our families to the cosmic belief that God will establish a new and perfect world. In this lesson, we examined the role of Jesus in God's plan. Jesus, standing fully within the Jewish tradition, announced that the God of Israel was preparing to bring about a transformed world. His message was specifically directed to the marginalized of society, of whom he was a part. In light of his resurrection, the early church began to proclaim the good news that God had begun to establish this kingdom through Jesus.

Christian faith, then, is believing in a God who has in fact raised Jesus from the dead as the first step in establishing a new creation. Christian hope is that God will complete the saving work that Jesus' resurrection began. It is our hope that God will bring about a world in which no one will be marginalized, because God will destroy every evil and make all things new. Our faith in Jesus, therefore, is inextricably connected to our hope in the world to come: "Amen! Come, Lord Jesus!" (Rev 22:20).

EXPLORING LESSON FOUR

1. What does it mean to say that Jesus had an apocalyptic worldview? How did this worldview affect the content of his preaching?

2. The commentary explores how the Our Father is really a prayer about the future. How might this perspective affect the way you pray the Our Father going forward?

3. Jesus ministered to those who were considered powerless or unimportant. Reflect on the stories you know of Jesus' ministry and his interactions with others. What example of his compassionate ministry is a favorite of yours and why?

4. Revisit the account of the Judgment of the Nations (Matt 25:31-46). How has God called you—or how might God be calling you—to serve those in need, in imitation of his own ministry?

5. Read one of the Gospel stories of healing mentioned in the section "Faith and Jesus' Healing Miracles" (p. 63). Do you personally relate to the story in any way? What insight about faith can you share from reflecting on this story?

6. Faith is a free gift from God, and yet Jesus encourages us to "have faith" (Mark 11:22) and "believe" (John 20:27). What role do we play in having faith?

7. In what way is worry the opposite of faith? What strategies do you use to worry less and trust God more?

8. How is Jesus' resurrection connected with the resurrection of all the dead (1 Cor 15:20-24)?

9. According to Jesus' own preaching, the kingdom of God is both a present and a future reality (e.g., Mark 4:30-32). Although God's reign will not be fulfilled until Jesus returns, how do you already perceive the kingdom of God "among you" (Luke 17:21)?

10. What insight about faith or hope can you share with your group after studying and reflecting on the New Testament texts explored in this lesson?

CLOSING PRAYER

Prayer

"Blessed are you who are poor, for the kingdom of God is yours." (Luke 6:20)

God of faith and hope, you have fully revealed yourself in your Son, Jesus Christ, who lived and preached a gospel of divine love for all people, especially the most vulnerable among us. Increase the gift of faith in us, so we may imitate the love and compassion of Christ, offering hope to all we meet, especially . . .

LESSON FIVE

God's Love for Us

Begin your personal study and group discussion with a simple and sincere prayer such as:

Prayer

Lord God, help us listen with the ears of our hearts as we spend time with your word. Reveal yourself to us today as you have revealed yourself through the ages, and strengthen in us your gifts of faith, hope, and love.

Read the pages 72–82, Lesson Five.

Respond to the questions on pages 83–85, Exploring Lesson Five.

The Closing Prayer on page 86 is for your personal use and may be used at the end of group discussion.

GOD'S LOVE FOR US

In the introduction to this study, faith, hope, and love were described as "three interconnected dimensions of the divine-human relationship." Faith was defined as "entering into and clinging to a personal relationship with God, who is recognized as trustworthy," and hope was understood as "what we expect from that relationship." Our first four lessons have traced how faith and hope developed as God's identity was revealed over time. God, who was first understood as the God of the Family, was over centuries revealed as the God who has begun to establish a new creation in Jesus Christ. In the last two lessons of our study, we will explore the third dimension of the triad that enables our relationship with God: love.

Faith and hope describe our side of the divine-human relationship. We believe and hope in order to participate in the covenant with God. Faith and hope do not pertain to God. God, who is all-knowing and all-powerful, has no need to believe or hope. Therefore, the only dimension of the triad that applies both to God and to us is love. Although God's love and our love are of a different order entirely, the term "love" can be expanded to indicate what both God and we contribute to the relationship between us.

In this lesson, we will explore how the Bible presents God's love for us. The Hebrew word that regularly expresses God's love in the Hebrew Scriptures is *hesed.* The root term was often used by rulers in the ancient Near East as they formed political covenants with each other. *Hesed* described what the more powerful party of the covenant would give to the weaker party. Because God is clearly the more powerful party in the divine-human relationship, *hesed* is a fitting word to name what God contributes. The word aptly conveys three factors of divine love: loyalty, help, and freedom. God is the One who loves faithfully, provides what is needed, and acts with complete sovereignty. These multiple nuances explain why scriptural translations can render *hesed* not only as "love" but also as "loving-kindness," "mercy," and "steadfast love."

The Greek word for love that is most often used by the writers of the New Testament is *agape.* When it refers to God's love, it carries the same characteristics as the Hebrew term *hesed.*

Our review of God's love in this lesson must necessarily be selective. But in the space permitted here, we will discover that the Bible presents God's love as inexplicable, scandalous, universal, and incarnate.

God's Inexplicable Love

We have already discussed how God freely initiated a relationship with human beings through Abraham. A question we have not addressed is *why* God initiated such a relationship. Why would God choose to establish a personal bond with humanity? It cannot be because God has any need for such a relationship. God is not lonely or bored. God is fully sufficient and in need of nothing. So what motivated God's call to Abraham, a call that led to a covenant with Israel and, ultimately, a new covenant offered to all people? The Bible attempts to answer this question, and the clearest answer it offers is love.

In 621 BCE, during the reign of Josiah, king of Judah, a "book of the law" was discovered in the Jerusalem temple (2 Kgs 22). This book was probably an early edition of the material now found in the book of Deuteronomy. It presented a distinctive understanding of Israel's covenant with God. For our purposes, the important contribution of this Deuteronomic material is its understanding of *why* God established a relationship with Israel. A crucial passage is found in Deuteronomy 7:

> *Deuteronomy 7:6-11*
>
> 6For you are a people holy to the LORD, your
> God; the LORD, your God, has chosen you from all the peoples on the face of the earth to be a people specially his own. 7It was not because you are more
> numerous than all the peoples that the LORD set his heart on you and chose you; for you are really the smallest of all peoples. 8It was because the LORD
> loved you and because of his fidelity to the oath he had sworn to your ancestors, that the LORD brought you out with a strong hand and redeemed you from the house of slavery, from the hand of Pharaoh, king of Egypt. 9Know, then, that the LORD, your God,
> is God: the faithful God who keeps covenant mercy to the thousandth generation toward those who love him and keep his commandments, 10but who
> repays with destruction those who hate him; he does not delay with those who hate him, but makes them pay for it. 11Therefore carefully observe the
> commandment, the statutes and the ordinances which I command you today.

These verses exhort readers and hearers to "carefully observe" God's commands (v. 11). Doing so will ensure blessings as part of the covenant (v. 9). Failure to obey will bring destruction (v. 10). Therefore, the focus of the passage is upon the human side of the divine-human relationship. But before calling for human obedience, this passage throws light on why God chose Israel to be "a people specially his own" (v. 6). It insists that the choice had nothing to do with Israel's size or achievements. In fact, the passage describes Israel as "the smallest of all peoples" (v. 7). This assertion may well be an overstatement, yet when Israel is compared to the great empires that surrounded it—Egypt, Babylonia, Assyria—the force of the claim rings true. God did not initiate the covenant because Israel was large or powerful.

Why, then, did God choose Israel? God is said to have "set his heart"—or "set his love"—upon Israel (v. 7). The Hebrew verb used here carries a remarkably physical sense. The same verb is used in Genesis 34:8 and Deuteronomy 21:11 to describe a man's physical attraction to a woman whom he desires as his wife. The motive of love becomes explicit in verse 8 when the simple explanation for God's choice is given: "[T]he LORD loved you." The text then connects this love to the oath given to Abraham ("your ancestors") and affirms how God's love was demonstrated through the exodus from Egypt.

Deuteronomy describes the love of God as a gift that will last. God is "the faithful God who keeps covenant mercy to the thousandth generation" (v. 9). Behind the expression "covenant mercy" is the Hebrew word *hesed*, which, as we have seen, can also be translated as "loving-kindness" or "steadfast love." Israel knows that God's "loving-kindness" is the reason for the covenant with God and that God's love will not end.

Love as the sole motivation for God's choice of Israel is repeated in another passage in Deuteronomy:

> *Deuteronomy 10:14-15*
>
> 14Look, the heavens, even the highest heavens, belong to the LORD, your God, as well as the earth and everything on it. 15Yet only on your ancestors
> did the LORD set his heart to love them. He chose you, their descendants, from all the peoples, as it is today.

God, the creator of all things, chose Israel because of love.

Contemporary Relevance. If we are serious about our relationship with God, we will try to give ourselves fully to that relationship. We worship God. We pray. We strive to follow God's commands. All of this is good and appropriate. But because so much of our time and energy is focused on our actions, we can begin to believe that what we do is more important than it really is. The viewpoint of Deuteronomy reminds us that our relationship with God is not based on our own actions or achievements, however good they may be. God freely chooses to relate to us because of God's inexplicable love.

This is especially important to remember when we have failed in our responsibilities to God. When we hurt someone deeply, when we give in to selfishness or manipulation, when we allow anger to rule our lives, we may conclude that God will reject us. But God does not love us because we are good. We are good because God loves us. It is because God has loved us first that we are able to follow God's commands.

If our relationship with God depended on us, it would soon end. But because the relationship is founded on God's steadfast love, it continues "to the thousandth generation" despite our weakness and sin (v. 9). So even when our obedience to God is partial or faulty, God's inexplicable love remains.

God's love for Israel is especially celebrated in the psalms. Israel worships the God who loves: "I look to you in the sanctuary / to see your power and glory. / For your love is better than life; / my lips shall ever praise you!" (Ps 63:3-4; see also Pss 57:11; 138:2). It is God's love that protects and saves the believer: "My strength, for you I watch; / you, God, are my fortress, / my loving God" (Ps 59:10-11; see also Pss 17:7; 36:8; 40:11-12; 94:18; 109:21). Many psalms emphasize the never-ending nature of God's love (89:2; 100:5; 117:2; 118:1-4).

But perhaps the most exuberant celebration of God's faithful love is found in Psalm 136. Each of its twenty-six verses ends with the Hebrew noun *hesed*. The translation below renders *hesed* as "mercy." It could just as accurately be translated as "love." The constant refrain suggests that this psalm was prayed in the Jerusalem temple in an antiphonal manner between cantor and chorus. The psalm is divided into six sections:

Psalm 136

I

1 Praise the LORD, for he is good;
for his mercy endures forever;
2 Praise the God of gods;
for his mercy endures forever;
3 Praise the Lord of lords;
for his mercy endures forever;

II

4 Who alone has done great wonders,
for his mercy endures forever;
5 Who skillfully made the heavens,
for his mercy endures forever;
6 Who spread the earth upon the waters,
for his mercy endures forever;
7 Who made the great lights,
for his mercy endures forever;
8 The sun to rule the day,
for his mercy endures forever;
9 The moon and stars to rule the night,
for his mercy endures forever;

III

10 Who struck down the firstborn of Egypt,
for his mercy endures forever;
11 And led Israel from their midst,
for his mercy endures forever;
12 With mighty hand and outstretched arm,
for his mercy endures forever;
13 Who split in two the Red Sea,
for his mercy endures forever;
14 And led Israel through its midst,
for his mercy endures forever;
15 But swept Pharaoh and his army into the Red Sea,
for his mercy endures forever;
16 Who led the people through the desert,
for his mercy endures forever;

IV

17 Who struck down great kings,
for his mercy endures forever;
18 Slew powerful kings,
for his mercy endures forever;

[19]Sihon, king of the Amorites,
for his mercy endures forever;
[20]Og, king of Bashan,
for his mercy endures forever;
[21]And made their lands a heritage,
for his mercy endures forever;
[22]A heritage for Israel, his servant,
for his mercy endures forever.

V

[23]The Lord remembered us in our low estate,
for his mercy endures forever;
[24]Freed us from our foes,
for his mercy endures forever;
[25]And gives bread to all flesh,
for his mercy endures forever.

VI

[26]Praise the God of heaven,
for his mercy endures forever.

From one section to the next, this psalm recounts God's everlasting love for Israel. Section I asserts that God is the only God. Section II recounts how God's love created the world. Section III ascribes the victory of the exodus to God's love. Section IV turns to the gift of the land (Sihon and Og were pagan kings who attempted to prevent Israel's settlement on the land but were defeated by God's *hesed*; see Num 21:21-35). Sections V and VI summarize the continuing action of God's love, describing how God saves Israel from its enemies and provides daily bread. The psalm echoes the claims of Deuteronomy 7:7-8 that, despite Israel's lowly estate (v. 23), God freely chose Israel with a love that endures.

By recognizing love as God's only motivation for establishing the divine-human relationship, both Deuteronomy and the psalms exclude any weakness or need on God's part. God did not form a covenant with human beings in order to receive anything from them. A relationship with God only exists because God freely chose for it to be. The best and perhaps only understanding humans can reach for why that choice was made is love. This love—for a people "specially [God's] own" (Deut 7:6) and for each one of us—ultimately remains inexplicable.

Of course, one could push the question further and ask why God loves us. But such a question only leads us deeper into the very mystery of God, which cannot be penetrated. As we stand before the profundity of God's own being, love is simply as far as our hearts and minds can reach.

Prayer Starter: The psalms were written to be prayed or sung out loud. Take some time to read Psalm 136 aloud—by yourself, with someone else, or with your Bible study group. What effect does the repetition have as you hear it out loud? What is the effect of speaking the psalm rather than praying it silently?

God's Scandalous Love

God is beyond our comprehension. God is invisible, inexpressible, ungraspable. God transcends creation and all creatures in it. Therefore, the only way to speak about God is through comparisons. Traits and qualities of human experience are applied to a God who transcends all of them. The technical term for this effort is *analogy*.

An analogy is a comparison between two realities. When applied to God, an analogy is a comparison between creator and creation, between the invisible and the visible, between what is ungraspable and what can be understood.

We cannot describe who God *is*; we can only say what God is *like*. God is *like* the goodness we see in our children or the beauty we find in nature. We may point to the best aspects of our lives and assert that they provide a glimpse of God. Yet even here the comparisons we draw are severely limited. Any comparison we make between God and the created world can capture an *aspect* of God's being, but an even larger dimension of God escapes us. We speak of God through analogies that not only limp but barely crawl.

Yet imperfect analogies are all we have. Without them we could say nothing about God. Using them allows us to describe some aspects of God's activity and identity, albeit in a limited way. Biblical analogies are particularly valuable to us because they derive from revered texts that we as believers hold as inspired by the Holy Spirit. The biblical authors, like all writers, drew upon images from their own experience when they spoke about God.

The **parables of Jesus** can be seen as analogies of the coming kingdom of God. Because God's kingdom is a reality beyond our imagining, Jesus uses parables to suggest what God's reign will be *like*. He employs concrete realities of this world, which can be seen and touched, to create a comparison to the world to come. God's kingdom is *like* a mustard seed (Mark 4:30-34) or a treasure buried in a field (Matt 13:44). In Jesus' parables the precise comparison to God's kingdom is elusive and never complete because—like every analogy applied to God—it can only hint at what is beyond our ability to grasp and understand.

Isaiah 49:15, for example, compares the depth of God's love to the love of a mother: "Can a mother forget her infant, / be without tenderness for the child of her womb? / Even should she forget, / I will never forget you." Isaiah 62:5 draws an analogy between the joy of God's love and the joy of a newly married couple: "For as a young man marries a virgin, / your Builder shall marry you; / And as a bridegroom rejoices in his bride / so shall your God rejoice in you."

As moving and effective as these comparisons are, their power is overshadowed by the shocking analogy offered to us by Hosea, a prophet who was active in the northern kingdom of Israel from 750 to 725 BCE. Hosea's preaching decried Israel's tendency to worship the gods of the surrounding Canaanite culture. What is most notable about Hosea's message is the intensely personal way he describes God's relationship with Israel and the scandalous analogy he uses to illustrate God's love.

The opening commission God gives to the prophet is certainly one of the most unexpected in the Bible: "Go, get for yourself a woman of prostitution and children of prostitution, for the land prostitutes itself, turning away from the LORD" (Hos 1:2). God is sending Hosea to marry a prostitute! The scandal of this command is magnified when we realize that prophets routinely performed actions that represented God's actions. Therefore, Hosea's marriage to a prostitute is meant to tell us something about God's love for Israel and, indeed, God's love for us.

Within the book of Hosea, prostitution refers both to immoral activity between humans and to the violation of a relationship with God through the worship of other gods. Hosea's scandalous marriage to Gomer, who has given herself to other lovers, expresses God's willingness to love and remain faithful to Israel despite Israel's own unfaithfulness.

Every analogy limps, but the image of marriage in the book of Hosea is particularly difficult for modern readers. Today we strive for a marriage of mutuality between partners. The book of Hosea, however, presumes male superiority within marriage (e.g., "get for yourself a woman"; 1:2). The husband chooses whom to marry and holds the dominant position within the relationship. As distasteful as this inequality may be to us, it is what makes Hosea's marriage image a suitable analogy to our relationship with God. Our covenant with God is not a union of equals. In contemporary culture, a husband is not the lord of his wife. But God is indeed Lord of us. Therefore, to appreciate the force of Hosea's analogy, we must focus on what it says about God's relationship with us.

And what it says is astounding. The most important word in Hosea's call is "Go." Hosea reveals a God who *goes*, who goes to those who turn away from the love God offers. God does not simply go to those who fornicate with false gods; God goes to wed them. What would motivate such a scandalous action? Hosea's answer is love—a love that defies morality and justice, a love that is not deserved or even fair, a wild and irrational love that outrages some even as it brings joy to others. God's love binds itself to the one who is disgraced and unworthy. God's steadfast love will not give up, even if its recipients have debased themselves and slept with other lovers.

There are other biblical passages that express God's unlimited love for us, but none carry the shock of Hosea's analogy. Hosea employs a marriage relationship to assert that God's love continues despite betrayal. Yet God's love does not dismiss the offending party from responsibility. There will be discipline for the one who is unfaithful. God's faithful love and the consequences of betrayal are both acknowledged in this amazing passage from Hosea 2:

Hosea 2:15-17

15I will punish her for the days of the Baals,
for whom she burnt incense,
When she decked herself out with her rings
and her jewelry,
and went after her lovers—
but me she forgot—oracle of the LORD.
16Therefore, I will allure her now;
I will lead her into the wilderness
and speak persuasively to her.
17Then I will give her the vineyards she had,
and the valley of Achor as a door of hope.
There she will respond as in the days of her
youth,
as on the day when she came up from the
land of Egypt.

Verse 15 is a verse of anger, describing betrayal by the one who "went after her lovers." When verse 16 begins with "Therefore," we expect condemnation to follow. But what we are given is sexual attraction: "I will allure her now." The Hebrew verb translated here as "allure" carries an erotic sense close to "seduce." By using betrayal in a marriage as an analogy for our relationship with God, Hosea draws upon one of the deepest violations in human experience. He does this to insist that God's love can overcome such violation.

The love of God that Hosea presents is profoundly complex. Within these few verses, it is both fury and attraction, both exasperation and sexual beguilement. Hosea asserts that even in God's anger, an erotic allurement remains. God is still attracted to the prostitute and still desires her. No matter how deeply we may have violated our relationship, Hosea wants us to know that God still burns with the desire to love us.

This analogy is perhaps the most daring in the Scriptures. God, of course, is not sexually attracted to us. But Hosea uses erotic language to speak analogously about God's paradoxical love. The prophet defiantly describes a divine love that is beyond any category of human love and is ultimately hidden in the mystery of God's own being. Anger, attraction, correction, and allurement are presented as multiple sparks from a fire we cannot see. With frail words drawn from human experience, Hosea dares us to catch a glimpse of God's scandalous love for us.

Like Hosea, the **Song of Songs** uses human love to draw an analogy with divine love. This collection of secular love songs extols the power and beauty of sensual desire. God is never mentioned in the Song of Songs, but both Jewish and Christian interpreters see the relationship between the young lovers in these songs as an illustration of God's love. God is a passionate lover who desires union with us.

God's Universal Love

The main focus of the Hebrew Bible is the covenant between God and Israel. Only occasionally does the Old Testament focus on God's relationship with non-Jews. We have already seen a foretaste of this wider focus when God promised Abraham that "[a]ll the families of the earth will find blessing in you" (Gen 12:3). But perhaps the clearest expression of God's love for those outside of Israel is found in the book of Jonah.

The story of Jonah is best understood as a parable. Like the parables of Jesus, it is intended to provoke us and challenge our thinking. The book is usually dated after the return of the Jewish people from exile (538 BCE). But the story the book presents takes place much earlier, before the fall of the northern kingdom (701 BCE). God sends Jonah to preach repentance to the city of Nineveh, the capital of the Assyrian empire. Assyria was a ruthless nation, dominating other peoples and routinely deporting entire cities after they were conquered. In fact, Assyria destroyed the northern kingdom of Israel, and the ten tribes that composed that kingdom were never heard from again.

Given this terrible history, Israelites hated Assyrians. The reason Jonah flees from God's command (and is for a while swallowed by a great fish) is that he does not want God to show the Assyrians mercy. Quoting from Exodus 34:6-7 (a passage we discussed in Lesson Two), Jonah says to God: "This is why I fled at first toward Tarshish. I knew that you are a gracious and merciful God, slow to anger, abounding in kindness, repenting of punishment" (Jonah 4:2). Jonah fears that this great mercy of God will be extended to the Assyrians.

When he finally goes to Nineveh, what Jonah fears takes place. The entire city repents, and God forgives those whom Jonah hates (3:6-10). Disgusted with the extent of God's love, Jonah encamps outside Nineveh to see whether God will change and replace mercy with punishment. As he waits, he takes delight in a gourd plant that shelters him from the sun. When the plant dies, he becomes angry and asks God for death (4:8). God's response to Jonah ends the book:

Jonah 4:10-11

[10]Then the LORD said, "You are concerned over the gourd plant which cost you no effort and which you did not grow; it came up in one night and in one night it perished. [11]And should I not be concerned over the great city of Nineveh, in which there are more than a hundred and twenty thousand persons who cannot know their right hand from their left, not to mention all the animals?"

The book of Jonah delivers its message with irony and humor. The great reality of God's universal love is conveyed by God pleading with an irascible prophet over a gourd plant.

God's Desire that All Be Saved

Although it bears Paul's name, the First Letter to Timothy was probably written by a follower of Paul after his death, possibly as late as 100 CE. If so, it would be one of the last writings of the New Testament, offering a final sweep of the gospel message.

The letter states that God "wills everyone to be saved and to come to knowledge of the truth" (2:4). The verses that follow can be read as an early Christian creed, echoing the Jewish *shema*: "For there is one God. / There is also one mediator between God and the human race, / Christ Jesus, himself human, / who gave himself as ransom for *all*" (2:5-6; emphasis added).

God's universal love, clearly expressed in the book of Jonah, is here extended to the saving work of Jesus, who came to save all people.

God's argument is purposely extreme: *Look, you care about a dead plant. Can't I care about 120,000 Ninevites?* God takes the side of the Ninevites, excusing them as helpless people who don't even know their right hand from their left. God's last words are a final attempt to win Jonah over: *You may hate Assyrians, but how about all their innocent animals?*

We are not given Jonah's response to God's argumentation, but God's point has been made. This penetrating story clearly illustrates that God's love is not limited or exclusive. It is universal, extending to every person God has created. (Not to mention all the animals!)

Contemporary Relevance. The book of Jonah is more than a fish story. It proclaims God's love for all people. In a world where terrorism and threats of war are always present and escalating, we can easily find ourselves dividing into opposing camps and adopting an "us versus them" attitude. In such an atmosphere, it is easy to stereotype entire nations, characterizing some as "good" and others as "bad." The book of Jonah reminds us that God is beyond the issues that divide humanity. Even though we may see some people as enemies, God only sees sons and daughters to be loved, forgiven, and saved.

There are times when we, like Jonah, may find ourselves in a standoff with God about who deserves love and mercy. We take sides. God does not. We consider people who agree with us to be intelligent and worthy of respect and those who disagree with us to be ignorant and unworthy of our attention. But God attends to everyone. We believe that when people do something wrong, they should be punished. But the book of Jonah tells us that God is not looking for punishment. God is looking for an opportunity to show mercy.

But there is more good news in the book of Jonah. Even if we fall into partisan and vengeful thinking, God does not reject us. Throughout the whole Jonah story, Jonah remains steadfast in his hatred of the Assyrians, but God does not reject him. God continues to guide Jonah, talk to him, and care for him. God will do the same for us. Even if we are unable to forgive, even if we are unwilling to consider another point of view, even if we are overcome with anger against our enemies, God does not give up on us. God keeps patiently calling us to change. God sits down with us and listens to our narrow complaints, sighing as we again express our anger over matters as petty as a gourd plant. God gives us time to grow, to embrace a love that extends not only to us but to all that God has made.

God's Incarnate Love

In Lesson Four we discussed how, with the death and resurrection of Jesus, the contours of faith and hope have changed. Faith is believing that God raised Jesus from the dead, and hope is the expectation that Jesus will return to establish God's kingdom. The New Testament writers consider the resurrection of Jesus to be the summit of God's action in the divine-human relationship. The good news they proclaim is that, in Jesus' resurrection, the final act of God—bringing about a new creation—has begun. Moreover, they understand that God's gift of Jesus was motivated by the same dynamic force that began the divine-human relationship in the first place. That force is love.

Saint Paul knows that the death and resurrection of Jesus result from God's love. In Romans 5:8 he says, "But God proves his love for us in that while we were still sinners Christ died for us." The letter to the Ephesians describes our present condition in Christ in a similar way: "In love he destined us for adoption to himself through Jesus Christ, in accord with the favor of his will" (1:4-5; see also 2:4-6).

Because Christ is essential to God's saving activity, Paul and other New Testament writers speak of God's love and Christ's love interchangeably. Christ's death and resurrection are at times said to be the result of Christ's love, as in Paul's declaration "I live, no longer I, but Christ lives in me; insofar as I now live in the flesh, I live by faith in the Son of God who has loved me and given himself up for me" (Gal 2:20).

God's love for us is often in the background as Paul proclaims the good news. In one particular passage, however, God's love seizes the spotlight. In discussing the numerous trials believers must face, Paul consoles his readers by offering a soaring exaltation of God's love:

> *Romans 8:31-39*
>
> 31What then shall we say to this? If God is for
> us, who can be against us? 32He who did not spare
> his own Son but handed him over for us all, how
> will he not also give us everything else along with
> him? 33Who will bring a charge against God's
> chosen ones? It is God who acquits us. 34Who will
> condemn? It is Christ [Jesus] who died, rather,
> was raised, who also is at the right hand of God,
> who indeed intercedes for us. 35What will separate
> us from the love of Christ? Will anguish, or distress, or persecution, or famine, or nakedness, or
> peril, or the sword? 36As it is written:
>
> "For your sake we are being slain all the day;
> we are looked upon as sheep to be
> slaughtered."
>
> 37No, in all these things we conquer overwhelmingly through him who loved us. 38For I am con-
> vinced that neither death, nor life, nor angels, nor
> principalities, nor present things, nor future things,
> nor powers, 39nor height, nor depth, nor any other
> creature will be able to separate us from the love of
> God in Christ Jesus our Lord.

Paul's central argument is that "God is for us" (v. 31). For proof he points to God's saving action in Christ, who was handed over for us (v. 32) and was raised up (v. 34). Paul insists that if God has done this for us, God will also give us whatever we need (v. 32).

Paul then repeats his argument on a deeper level, this time referring explicitly to love. God is for us because of love—the love of Christ—and nothing can separate us from it (v. 35). Christ's love is another way of referring to God's love, a shorthand for expressing "the love of God in Christ Jesus our Lord" (v. 39). All that has happened in Christ is the result of God's love (v. 37). This love is the same love that moved God to speak to Abraham. It is *hesed*—enduring love. Nothing can break the bond that God's love has made.

The Gospel of John gives witness to God's love in a verse known even to those who do not read the Bible: "For God so loved the world that he gave his only Son, so that everyone who believes in him might not perish but might have eternal life" (3:16). This verse clearly asserts that the love God has for us is given preeminent expression in Jesus. It echoes the great prologue that begins John's Gospel, a portion of which is excerpted here:

> *John 1:1, 14, 18*
>
> 1In the beginning was the Word,
> and the Word was with God,
> and the Word was God.
>
> 14And the Word became flesh
> and made his dwelling among us,
> and we saw his glory,
> the glory as of the Father's only Son,
> full of grace and truth.
>
> 18No one has ever seen God. The only Son, God,
> who is at the Father's side, has revealed him.

The preexisting Word of God has been enfleshed in the human condition and has become the communication between God and us. The ultimate expression of God's love, then, is to be found in a person. This is incarnate love—a love given to us in the Eternal Word who now dwells among us. The Word displays the glory of the Father's only Son, which is "full of grace and truth" (v. 14). The two terms here translated as "grace and truth" are Greek parallels to the two Hebrew words used to describe God in Exodus 34:6—a God of "love [*hesed*] and fidelity." As such, they are yet another expression of God's covenant relationship with Israel. Jesus, then, is the embodiment of God's enduring, covenant love.

Throughout the Gospel of John, God's incarnate love is expressed in terms of a father-son relationship. The love of the Father is shared with the Son. As Jesus explains: "For the Father loves his Son and shows him everything that he himself does, and he will show him greater works than these, so that you may be amazed" (5:20; see also 3:35; 10:17). The Son, in turn, shares the Father's love with those who believe in him: "For the Father himself loves you, because you have loved me and have come to believe that I came from God" (16:27; see also 14:21, 23). God's love is incarnate, reaching us through the person of Jesus.

This unity between the Father, the Son, and believers is stated most forcibly in John 17, which is often called Jesus' "high priestly prayer." In it, Jesus prays to the Father for his disciples. Here is the conclusion of the prayer:

John 17:20-26

20"I pray not only for them, but also for those
who will believe in me through their word, 21so
that they may all be one, as you, Father, are in me
and I in you, that they also may be in us, that the
world may believe that you sent me. 22And I have
given them the glory you gave me, so that they may
be one, as we are one, 23I in them and you in me,
that they may be brought to perfection as one, that
the world may know that you sent me, and that
you loved them even as you loved me. 24Father,
they are your gift to me. I wish that where I am
they also may be with me, that they may see my
glory that you gave me, because you loved me before the foundation of the world. 25Righteous
Father, the world also does not know you, but I
know you, and they know that you sent me. 26I
made known to them your name and I will make
it known, that the love with which you loved me
may be in them and I in them."

Jesus prays that his disciples and those who believe in him based on their word will be one as he is one with the Father (v. 21). In other words, he prays that those who believe in him will share in the unity God has with the Son.

In verse 23 it becomes clear that this unity is one of love. This love God has had for the Son since the foundation of the world is now extended to believers (v. 24). John asserts that believers can participate in the very life of the Father and Son, a life that is one of love (v. 26). God's *hesed*, God's enduring love, has been made available to us through the Word made flesh.

Another New Testament work, the First Letter of John, was written after the Gospel of John, around 100 CE. It adopts the same understanding of God's love that is present in the Gospel, describing the saving events of Christ's incarnation, death, and resurrection as motivated by God's love: "In this way the love of God was revealed to us: God sent his only Son into the world so that we might have life through him" (4:9; see also 3:1, 16). First John also emphasizes the priority of God's love: "In this is love: not that we have loved God, but that he loved us and sent his Son as expiation for our sins" (4:10). But perhaps the most significant contribution this letter makes to our understanding of God's love is crystallized in one verse: "We have come to know and to believe in the love God has for us. God is love, and whoever remains in love remains in God and God in him" (4:16; see also 4:8).

Here, with insight and simplicity, 1 John 4:16 summarizes the entire discussion of this lesson. Why did God initiate a relationship with Abraham, lead Israel out of Egypt, make Israel a great nation, bring Israel out of exile, promise a new world, and initiate it through the resurrection of Jesus? Not simply because God is loving, but because God is love. Deep within the person of God, which we can never penetrate, there is a love that reaches out to establish a relationship with all the creatures God has made. It is an enduring love, a love that is most fully expressed in the incarnation of the Eternal Word.

Contemporary Relevance. In Jesus, God has achieved the ultimate expression of love. God's love for humanity has been real and effective from the beginning of time. Yet Christ's incarnate love pushes God's relationship with us to its most personal and immediate expression.

Two people in love can successfully maintain a long-distance relationship. Living in different cities, they can remain connected through texts, phone calls, and video calls. If their love is real, it can flourish and grow even when they are apart. Yet nothing can replace the moments in their relationship when they can meet in person and stand in each other's presence. When we are ill or recovering from a serious operation, those who love us express their care through cards, messages, and thoughtful gifts. The love they offer us is genuine, providing support and strengthening our courage. But such expressions are qualitatively different from those of a friend who enters our home, sits by our bedside, and personally holds our hand.

God, who freely initiated a relationship with humanity through Abraham, was serious about loving us from the start. But in Christ, God's love broke through all limitations of space and time. In the incarnate love of Jesus, God does more than care and provide for us. God loves us in person.

EXPLORING LESSON FIVE

1. According to Deuteronomy 7:6-11, why did God choose Israel to be "a people specially his own"? Why is this surprising or inexplicable?

2. Reflect on Psalm 136. Which verse or image resonates with you the most from this psalm about God's *hesed*? Why?

3. Because we cannot accurately say what God *is*, we use analogies to say what God is *like*. Write your own analogy about God beginning, "God is like . . ." What aspect of God does your analogy capture? How is it limited?

4. Though any analogy fails to capture the full truth about God, Hosea's analogy is inspired Scripture. How does this scandalous analogy speak to you as you witness God's love for you, for others, and for our world?

5. a) Why doesn't Jonah want to preach repentance to the people of Nineveh (Jonah 1:1-3; 3:10–4:2)?

   b) Have you ever fled "away from the LORD" (Jonah 1:3) when God asked you to show compassion to someone that you felt did not deserve it? How did you come to accept and do God's will in that situation?

6. What does it mean to say that God's love has become "incarnate" in Jesus (John 1:1-18)?

7. What insight(s) about God's love do you gain from the way Jesus talks about his relationship with the Father and with believers in his high priestly prayer (John 17:20-26)?

8. We tend to take for granted the statement: "God is love" (1 John 4:16). How have you experienced this profound reality in an incarnate, "in-person" way?

9. What insight about God's love can you share with your group after studying and reflecting on the Scripture texts explored in this lesson?

CLOSING PRAYER

Prayer

For I am convinced that neither death, nor life, nor angels, nor principalities, nor present things, nor future things, nor powers, nor height, nor depth, nor any other creature will be able to separate us from the love of God in Christ Jesus our Lord. (Rom 8:38-39)

God of love, you have revealed your love to us through the ages as pure gift, freely and generously given to your people, even when we fail to respond in kind. May your love, which has been poured into our hearts through the Spirit of Christ (Rom 5:5), strengthen us to love one another. Today we pray for those most in need of your love and ours, especially . . .

LESSON SIX

Our Love for God

Begin your personal study and group discussion with a simple and sincere prayer such as:

Prayer

Lord God, help us listen with the ears of our hearts as we spend time with your word. Reveal yourself to us today as you have revealed yourself through the ages, and strengthen in us your gifts of faith, hope, and love.

Read pages 88–97, Lesson Six.

Respond to the questions on pages 98–100, Exploring Lesson Six.

The Closing Prayer on page 100 is for your personal use and may be used at the end of group discussion.

OUR LOVE FOR GOD

In the previous lesson, we examined how the Bible presents God's love for us. In this final lesson, we will explore our love for God.

What does it mean to love God? The question is not a simple one. Both we and God engage in love, but what does our love contribute to the relationship? We cannot and do not provide anything that God needs. God is complete. God does not depend on our love. What, then, is our love for God meant to accomplish? Exploring this question is the goal of this lesson.

The Hebrew Scriptures: Transferred Love

Worship is clearly one way to express our love for God. The psalmist writes, "But I, through the abundance of your mercy, / will enter into your house. / I will bow down toward your holy sanctuary / out of fear of you" (Ps 5:8). In this context "fear" should be understood as "awe." The Hebrew word that is here translated as "mercy" is *hesed,* which as we have seen is the word used to describe God's love. The psalmist approaches God's sanctuary with awe to return love for love (see also Pss 26:8; 84:2-3).

But love for God is more than worshipping God. The book of Deuteronomy broadens our understanding. Deuteronomy 6:4-5 is the fulcrum around which the entire book revolves:

Deuteronomy 6:4-5

4Hear, O Israel! The LORD is our God, the
LORD alone! 5Therefore, you shall love the LORD,
your God, with your whole heart, and with your
whole being, and with your whole strength.

Verse 4 calls Israel to "[h]ear," to recognize that "[t]he LORD is *our* God" (emphasis added). This verse thereby reminds us of the covenant initiated with Abraham, the divine-human relationship made possible through faith and hope. Aware of this bond, verse 5 begins with "Therefore," clearly indicating a response: "Therefore, you shall love the LORD, your God." If faith and hope enable the relationship between God and us, the resulting bond is to be expressed through our love.

Verse 5 continues, asserting that the love we offer to God must be of our whole heart, being, and strength. These three dimensions refer to everything we are. If God contributes to the divine-human relationship by loving us, we are to contribute by loving God in response and doing so completely.

We must resist understanding the love we are to offer God in a romanticized way. In our culture, love is often understood as an emotion. When we "fall in love," we submit to a feeling. Loving God in the biblical tradition is much more than emotion. As Deuteronomy makes clear, it includes everything we are. It is how we give our whole selves to the relationship with God.

In what, then, does our loving consist? Deuteronomy continues to guide us:

Deuteronomy 10:12-19

12Now, therefore, Israel, what does the LORD,
your God, ask of you but to fear the LORD, your

God, to follow in all his ways, to love and serve
the LORD, your God, with your whole heart and
with your whole being, [13]to keep the command-
ments and statutes of the LORD that I am com-
manding you today for your own well-being?
[14]Look, the heavens, even the highest heavens,
belong to the LORD, your God, as well as the earth
and everything on it. [15]Yet only on your ancestors
did the LORD set his heart to love them. He chose
you, their descendants, from all the peoples, as it
is today. [16]Circumcise therefore the foreskins of
your hearts, and be stiff-necked no longer. [17]For
the LORD, your God, is the God of gods, the Lord
of lords, the great God, mighty and awesome, who
has no favorites, accepts no bribes, [18]who executes
justice for the orphan and the widow, and loves
the resident alien, giving them food and clothing.
[19]So you too should love the resident alien, for
that is what you were in the land of Egypt.

If we had to select one passage from the Hebrew Scriptures to understand our love for God, this would be the passage to choose. Verse 12 clearly echoes Deuteronomy 6:4-5: We are to love God with our whole being. But this verse also elaborates on what loving God means. We are to "follow in all his ways." Following God's ways is doing what God expects, keeping God's commands (v. 13). This is our contribution to the covenant with God. Verses 14-15 remind us again that God acted first and "set his heart to love" Israel. We are called, then, to mirror that love by loving in return.

But most importantly for our purposes, this passage draws a clear connection between who God is and how we are to offer love to God. Verse 18 reminds us that God is the executor of justice for the "orphan and the widow" and the lover of the "resident alien." Because God loves these marginalized members of society, we are called to love them also (v. 19).

Here we uncover a crucial aspect of our love for God in the Bible. God has loved us first, and we are expected to return God's love. But God does not need our love. So God asks us to direct it to those who do. We will call this *transferred love.* God does not benefit from or need our love, but the widow, orphan, and resident alien do. God asks us to transfer love to them, to express our love for God through our love for others. This ties love of God and love of others closely together. They are two expressions of one and the same action of love.

The demand to love others in this way is not limited to Deuteronomy. A series of ancient laws in chapters 18–20 of the book of Leviticus are addressed to all Israelites as a way to live as a holy people in relationship with the Lord. This passage from Leviticus 19 commands love of neighbor:

Leviticus 19:17-18

[17]You shall not hate any of your kindred in
your heart. Reprove your neighbor openly so that
you do not incur sin because of that person.
[18]Take no revenge and cherish no grudge against
your own people. You shall love your neighbor as
yourself. I am the LORD.

Another passage from Leviticus 19 applies the same command to non-Israelites residing within Israelite territory:

Leviticus 19:33-34

[33]When an alien resides with you in your land,
do not mistreat such a one. [34]You shall treat the
alien who resides with you no differently than the
natives born among you; you shall love the alien
as yourself; for you too were once aliens in the
land of Egypt. I, the LORD, am your God.

These laws command love toward one's neighbor and toward the resident alien because Israel is in covenant with God ("I, the LORD, am your God"; v. 34). This once again is *transferred love*: love of others—especially the marginalized—as the way to love God.

The *Catechism of the Catholic Church* acknowledges the importance of **transferred love** when it describes charity as "the theological virtue by which we love God above all things for his own sake, and our neighbor as ourselves for the love of God" (1822). It also reminds us that "love of neighbor is inseparable from love of God" (1878).

The prophet Hosea intensifies this understanding of love through an unexpected use of vocabulary. As we have already noted, *hesed* is the preferred Hebrew word to describe God's love for us. *Hesed* was a word often used in covenants between rulers in the ancient Near East, describing the aid that the powerful party would provide for the weaker member of the relationship. This makes *hesed* a perfect word to describe God's love because God is clearly the superior party in the divine-human relationship. Yet when Hosea describes what we must do for God, he uses *hesed* six times to describe *our* contribution to the relationship: "For it is loyalty [*hesed*] that I desire, not sacrifice, / and knowledge of God rather than burnt offerings" (6:6; see also 2:21; 4:1; 6:4; 10:12; 12:7). To speak of our love for God as *hesed* is unexpected and must have confused Hosea's listeners. How can we, the weaker party in the relationship, offer *hesed* to God?

Transferred love provides a context in which this question can be answered. When we return God's love by the love, loyalty, kindness, and mercy we extend to others, we act as God acts. In the divine-human relationship, God is the giver. When we give what we have to others, we take up the role of giver, imitating God's giving. To this extent our love can be seen as *hesed*. Freely providing good to our neighbor mirrors the *hesed* of God, who has provided us with everything. Through our love of others, we love God and thereby fulfill our responsibility within the covenant.

The Hebrew Scriptures display a robust understanding of our love for God, uniting it to our love of others and asserting that the love we show others is ultimately rooted in the love God first extended to us. Loving others is loving God.

Contemporary Relevance. Christians have a tendency to set the Hebrew Scriptures and the New Testament against each other. The Old Testament is characterized as a book of law, judgment, and punishment, and the New Testament is exalted as an expression of forgiveness, mercy, and love. One of the aims of this study has been to demonstrate how the forgiveness and love found in the New Testament derive from the Hebrew Scriptures. What we have between the two testaments is not divergence but continuity.

This false opposition between testaments can also skew our understanding of Jesus. Because Jesus is, for us, the unique gift of God, our Messiah, there is a tendency to view everything about him as unique. This tendency overlooks his Jewishness and his deep dependence on and commitment to the Torah and the prophets. As we have just seen, the Hebrew Scriptures understand our love for others as love for God. Therefore, when Jesus commands us to love both God and neighbor, he is not introducing an original teaching. Jesus accepts and builds upon the understanding of love in the Jewish tradition. When he bases his teaching on love, he does so because he is a Jew.

The Great Commandment of Jesus

Jesus' emphasis on love is expressed most clearly in his Great Commandment, which is found in all three Synoptic Gospels (Matt 22:36-40; Mark 12:28-34; Luke 10:25-28). Here is Mark's version:

Mark 12:28-34

The Greatest Commandment. 28One of the scribes, when he came forward and heard them

> disputing and saw how well he had answered them, asked him, "Which is the first of all the commandments?" 29Jesus replied, "The first is this: 'Hear, O Israel! The Lord our God is Lord alone! 30You shall love the Lord your God with all your heart, with all your soul, with all your mind, and with all your strength.' 31The second is this: 'You shall love your neighbor as yourself.' There is no other commandment greater than these." 32The scribe said to him, "Well said, teacher. You are right in saying, 'He is One and there is no other than he.' 33And 'to love him with all your heart, with all your understanding, with all your strength, and to love your neighbor as yourself' is worth more than all burnt offerings and sacrifices." 34And when Jesus saw that [he] answered with understanding, he said to him, "You are not far from the kingdom of God." And no one dared to ask him any more questions.

The setting for this passage is important. In the Gospels, Jesus often debates with fellow Jews in a hostile manner. But in this passage, we have two Jewish teachers (Jesus and a scribe) discussing the law in a positive, productive way. The scribe—appreciating how well Jesus argued the law (v. 28)—asks Jesus which is the first of the commandments. Jesus answers (vv. 29-31). The scribe commends Jesus on his position and repeats Jesus' answer, adding his own emphasis (vv. 32-33). Jesus responds to the scribe's additions with praise (v. 34). The scene is respectful and life-giving, two rabbis discussing what God expects of them.

Jesus' answer to the scribe is thoroughly Jewish. Rabbis regularly linked two scriptural texts for mutual interpretation if they shared a common word or phrase. Highlighting the shared phrase "you shall love" in both Deuteronomy 6:5 and Leviticus 19:18, Jesus unites the two commands: "You shall love the Lord your God" and "You shall love your neighbor." He adds: "There is no other commandment greater than these" (vv. 30-31).

Here Jesus is carrying forward and reiterating the tradition of love that is expressed in the Hebrew Bible. In this sense, Jesus' Great Commandment does not break new ground. It is a thoughtful and effective expression of the connection already established, the connection of *transferred love*. We are to love God by loving our neighbor. Together, these two commandments form one Great Commandment.

In Matthew's version of the Great Commandment, a slight difference in wording tightens this connection even more. In Mark, after identifying the first commandment as loving God, Jesus says, "The second *is this*: 'You shall love your neighbor as yourself'" (Mark 12:31, emphasis added). But in the parallel verse in Matthew, Jesus instead says, "The second *is like it*: You shall love your neighbor as yourself" (Matt 22:39, emphasis added). "Like" can also be translated "the same as," making these two commands to love God and neighbor clear reflections of each other.

> Jewish rabbis often employed a teaching technique known as *gezera shawa*, in which similarities between unrelated texts were used to better understand both passages. Jesus' Great Commandment is an impressive example. In the entire Hebrew Bible, there are only four occurrences of the exact phrase "and you shall love . . ." (Lev 19:18, 34; Deut 6:5; 11:1). Jesus combines two of these occurrences in the Great Commandment. Clearly, **Rabbi Jesus** was very familiar with the precise wording of the Hebrew text.

The early church took the commonality of these two commands for granted. Saint Paul is even willing to say, "For the *whole law* is fulfilled in one statement, namely, 'You shall love your neighbor as yourself'" (Gal 5:14, emphasis added; see also Rom 13:8-9; cf. Jas 2:8). Has Paul forgotten the command to love God? Certainly not. Paul would be the last person to deny our obligation to love God. But here he does not feel the need to explicitly say it. Our love for God is simply "like"—the same as—loving our neighbor.

Jesus teaching by the seashore (James Tissot)

In his version of the Great Commandment, Luke explores how far the term "neighbor" should extend. After Jesus states the command to love God and neighbor in Luke 10:26-28, the legal scholar with whom he is speaking asks him, "And who is my neighbor?" Jesus responds with the parable of the Good Samaritan, a story in which a Samaritan stops to help a Jew who has fallen victim to robbers (10:29-37). When the story ends, Jesus asks who was "neighbor" to the Jewish victim (10:36). The answer the scholar gives is correct: "The one who treated him with mercy" (10:37). In Luke's Gospel, Jesus clearly enlarges the understanding of "neighbor" to extend beyond members of our own family, nation, or race. Anyone in need is our neighbor. And loving them is loving God.

Jesus' Command to Love Our Enemy

A second passage in the Synoptic Gospels that is crucial to understanding our love for God is Jesus' command to love our enemies. At first it may seem that this command is not relevant to our inquiry, because God is not mentioned in the command itself. But this challenging teaching of Jesus' is intimately connected to our love for God.

The command is found in Matthew 5:43-48 and Luke 6:27-36. Here is Matthew's version:

Matthew 5:43-48

Love of Enemies. 43"You have heard that it was
said, 'You shall love your neighbor and hate your
enemy.' 44But I say to you, love your enemies, and
pray for those who persecute you, 45that you may
be children of your heavenly Father, for he makes
his sun rise on the bad and the good, and causes
rain to fall on the just and the unjust. 46For if you
love those who love you, what recompense will you
have? Do not the tax collectors do the same? 47And
if you greet your brothers only, what is unusual
about that? Do not the pagans do the same? 48So
be perfect, just as your heavenly Father is perfect.

In this passage, Matthew is using the literary form of *antithesis*. In using this literary form, he sets the teaching of Jesus against what came before it ("You have heard that it was said"; v. 43) to reveal what Jesus expects of us ("But I say to you"; v. 44). Because the teaching before Jesus was the Jewish Torah, Matthew's use of antithesis has sometimes led to the false presumption that whatever is included in the first part is quoted from the Hebrew Scriptures. But this is not always the case.

Consider verse 43 above. The command to love one's neighbor is indeed a citation of Leviticus 19:18, as we have seen. But there is no command in the Hebrew Bible to hate one's enemy. There is instead a definite thread directing God's people to act with mercy toward an enemy. Here is a good example: "When you come upon your enemy's ox or donkey going astray, you must see to it that it is returned. When you notice the donkey of one who hates you lying down under its burden, you should not desert him; you must help him with it" (Exod 23:4-5; see also Prov 24:17-18, 29). Therefore, when Jesus tells his audience that they have heard they are to hate their enemy, he is referring not to a Jewish law but, rather, to a common human attitude found in every culture.

Jesus builds upon this already-existing biblical thread of *showing kindness* to enemies and says something new: His explicit, unconditioned command to *love* your enemies (v. 44) is unprecedented. Only Jesus commands us to love an enemy in such an unconditioned way. Placed as it is next to the command to "love your neighbor" (v. 43), Jesus is expanding our understanding of "neighbor" in the broadest way possible. Even our enemy is our neighbor. Therefore, even our enemy is to be loved.

Many of us do not have **literal "enemies."** But Jesus' teaching still has application for us. Any time we are irritated by someone, disagree with someone, are tempted to hold a grudge, or look down on someone for any reason, we can remember Jesus' call to love even those we find hardest to love.

Jesus' command to love our enemy is absolute. No conditions are attached to it. Nor does it promise practical results. There is no suggestion that our enemy will love us in return or become our friend. Even when we remember that Jesus is not commanding the emotion of love, the demand that we love our enemy—that we do good to and pray for the one we hate and who hates us—is overwhelming. We are to extend love to everyone, without concern for circumstances or results.

What is the reason for this absolute command to love? Its origin is found in our relationship with God. Verse 45 reveals that we are to love in this way so "that [we] may be children of [our] heavenly Father." Jesus here connects his teaching to our covenant relationship with God—the relationship initiated and maintained by God's everlasting *hesed.* God's love extends to *all.* God makes the sun shine and the rain fall on the bad and good, the just and unjust (v. 45). Because God's love is not limited or conditioned, we who stand in relationship with God must imitate this unqualified love.

Jesus then doubles down on this demand: "So be perfect, just as your heavenly Father is perfect" (v. 48). The word translated here as "perfect" can mean "mature," "whole," or "all-inclusive." We must determine the meaning from the word's context. Luke's version of this verse is helpful: "Be merciful, just as [also] your Father is merciful" (6:36). In the word "merciful," we hear again an allusion to God's everlasting *hesed.* The command of Jesus is to love totally, without limit, because that is how God loves.

We should admit up front that loving an enemy will only make sense to a person of faith. Only when we understand the limitless scope of God's love for us can we begin to understand what Jesus is asking of us—and why. We, of course, are not able to love as God loves. But if we are to stand in covenant relationship with God, if we are to make our response to the love God has shown us, we cannot impose limits on our love. Our love for God is *transferred love.* Here Jesus insists that we transfer it even to our enemy.

The command to love our enemy makes our love of others universal. If we are to love our enemy, there is no one left to exclude from our love. We will, of course, never love our enemy easily or well. But this is the command against which our love for God will be measured.

The Johannine Writings: A New Commandment of Love

The Johannine writings (the Gospel of John and the Letters of John) agree with the Synoptic Gospels that our love for God is to be expressed in our love for others. In John's Gospel, Jesus emphasizes the intimate bond between himself and the Father with clear statements such as "The Father and I are one" (John 10:30; see also 14:23). Loving God and loving Jesus are therefore the same love. That love is expressed in following Jesus' commands: "Whoever has my commandments and observes them is the one who loves me" (John 14:21).

The Gospel of John contains few ethical demands. Unlike the Synoptic Gospels, there are no teachings on fasting, divorce, or taxes. But one command Jesus does give in John is the command to love: His disciples are to love one another. This command is first expressed in an action. On the night before Jesus dies, he washes the feet of his disciples (John 13:1-17). This gesture is not a practical kindness. It is a sign of Jesus' supreme act of love in sacrificing himself for us. The foot washing is a model for the way his disciples are to love (13:15). The meaning of the foot washing is turned into a command: "I give you a new commandment: love one another. As I have loved you, so you also should love one another" (13:34; see also 15:12, 17).

This "new commandment" certainly stands in the tradition of *transferred love*. We are to love God and Jesus by loving one another. The logic of Jesus' command follows this path: We love God by loving Jesus (10:30). We love Jesus by keeping his command (14:21). His command is that we love one another (13:34). This is John's version of *transferred love*.

The First Letter of John follows the Gospel of John in its understanding of love. Our love of one another is required by Jesus' love for us: "The way we came to know love was that he laid down his life for us; so we ought to lay down our lives for our brothers" (1 John 3:16; see also 3:23). The letter also cites Jesus' command: "This is the commandment we have from him: whoever loves God must also love his brother" (4:21). The love of God and the love of others cannot be separated: "If anyone says, 'I love God,' but hates his brother, he is a liar; for whoever does not love a brother whom he has seen cannot love God whom he has not seen" (4:20). The First Letter of John is consistent with the rest of the Johannine tradition: We are to love God and love Jesus by transferring our love to one another.

When Jesus gives his commandment in John's Gospel, he calls it "a new commandment." If loving God through loving others is already well established in the tradition, how is Jesus' command new? The innovation of the new commandment is that Jesus sets himself as the standard for our love: "*As I have loved you*, so you also should love" (13:34, emphasis added). The newness of Jesus' command is daunting. Jesus raises the bar on love. After all, how does Jesus love us? John 15:13 says, "No one has greater love than this, to lay down one's life for one's friends." Jesus lays down his life for us and asks us to do the same for others.

It is logical to ask whether we can actually love at Jesus' level. Are we really able to lay down our lives as Jesus demands? A passage from the last chapter of John's Gospel, known as the epilogue, may help us address this valid question. In this account, the risen Jesus appears to his disciples as they fish in the Sea of Tiberias. He shares a meal with them on the beach, and then the following dialogue with the apostle Peter takes place:

John 21:15-17

Jesus and Peter. 15When they had finished breakfast, Jesus said to Simon Peter, "Simon, son of John, do you love me more than these?" He said to him, "Yes, Lord, you know that I love you." He said to him, "Feed my lambs." 16He then said to him a second time, "Simon, son of John, do you love me?" He said to him, "Yes, Lord, you know that I love you." He said to him, "Tend my sheep." 17He said to him the third time, "Simon, son of John, do you love me?" Peter was distressed that he had said to him a third time, "Do you love me?" and he said to him, "Lord, you know everything; you know that I love you." [Jesus] said to him, "Feed my sheep.

Jesus questions Peter three times. This triple questioning corresponds to the three times Peter denied Jesus during his passion (18:15-18, 25-27). This scene, then, is one of reconciliation, a new beginning. But it is also a dialogue about love. Peter is asked whether he is now willing to follow Jesus' new commandment. Can he love as Jesus loves? If he can, he will be able to assume Jesus' role as shepherd and feed Jesus' sheep. But to love like Jesus is to love at a very high level. It is to lay down one's life for the sheep (10:11). The high demands of the new commandment are clearly in play.

Yet this passage also provides a way in which the high demands of the new commandment may be conditioned. In the Greek text, there is an interesting fluctuation of verbs as Jesus and Peter use different words to describe love. The first two times Jesus asks, "Do you love me?" he uses the Greek verb *agapaó*. This is the same verb used in all three occurrences of Jesus' new commandment (13:34; 15:12, 17). Jesus is clearly asking Peter to love him by loving others as Jesus has loved them.

But Peter does not seem to catch this sense —or he may be trying to dodge it. In his first response to Jesus, he uses a different verb for love: *phileó*. Perhaps Peter is saying, "I am willing to love you, but not quite to the extent you command." Jesus and Peter then repeat this pattern a second time, using the same verbs. Neither of them budges. But in the third round, Jesus concedes. He uses Peter's verb, *phileó*, and the dialogue ends.

Peter does not change his vocabulary, but Jesus does. This shift may be an acknowledgment that we are not always able to live up to the high standard of the new commandment. When we cannot match the love of Jesus, he will accept the love that we can give.

Contemporary Relevance. We often fall short of the high expectations Jesus' new commandment places on us. We want to be understanding toward our spouse, present to our children, attentive to our aging parents. We strive to be flexible as we manage others in the workplace. But in one circumstance after another, our love does not rise to the goals we set. We not only fail to lay down our lives for others but sometimes even run from those who need our help.

When we are tempted to give in to discouragement, Jesus' dialogue with Peter can offer us hope. Jesus was willing to use Peter's word for love rather than his own. He sets aside what he asked of Peter and accepts the love that Peter is able to give. It is not far-fetched to conclude that Jesus will do the same for us. When our love does not rise to the high bar the new commandment has set, Jesus may be willing to accept the love we have to offer rather than judge us for the love we lack.

We may not have the strength to lay down our lives for others, but Jesus has indeed laid down his life for all of us. And the immensity of his sacrifice can cover our shortcomings and give us space to love as we are able. It might not be love at the highest level, but it is still loving God by loving others in Jesus' name.

Paul: Love as the Greatest Gift

Love is central in the letters of the apostle Paul. Like John, Paul also stresses the importance of loving one another, as he does in this passage from Romans 13:

Romans 13:8-10

Love Fulfills the Law. 8Owe nothing to anyone, except to love one another; for the one who loves another has fulfilled the law. 9The commandments, "You shall not commit adultery; you shall not kill; you shall not steal; you shall not covet," and whatever other commandment there may be, are summed up in this saying, [namely] "You shall love your neighbor as yourself." 10Love does no evil to the neighbor; hence, love is the fulfillment of the law.

This is Paul's expression of what we have called *transferred love*. Living God's law is an expression of our love for God. And if we desire to fulfill the law of God, we must love our neighbor.

When Paul speaks of love, he does not always distinguish between God's love for us and our love for God. Paul sees love as a dynamic unity, the constant giving and receiving from God to us and us to God and one another. "Love" is the term to describe the life that passes among us, a force that includes both sides of the divine-human covenant.

This perspective is present in Paul's most famous passage on love: 1 Corinthians 13:1-13. Paul is writing to the church in Corinth because he's heard of rivalries within the community (1 Cor 1:11). He uses the image of the body to show how their spiritual gifts are meant to work for the good of all (12:12-31a). Then Paul pivots to another argument: "But I shall show you a still more excellent way" (12:31b). What pours out next is the most exalted passage on love in the New Testament:

1 Corinthians 13:1-13

[1]If I speak in human and angelic tongues but
do not have love, I am a resounding gong or a
clashing cymbal. [2]And if I have the gift of prophecy
and comprehend all mysteries and all knowledge;
if I have all faith so as to move mountains but do
not have love, I am nothing. [3]If I give away every-
thing I own, and if I hand my body over so that I
may boast but do not have love, I gain nothing.
[4]Love is patient, love is kind. It is not jealous,
[love] is not pompous, it is not inflated, [5]it is not
rude, it does not seek its own interests, it is not
quick-tempered, it does not brood over injury, [6]it
does not rejoice over wrongdoing but rejoices
with the truth. [7]It bears all things, believes all
things, hopes all things, endures all things.
[8]Love never fails. If there are prophecies, they
will be brought to nothing; if tongues, they will
cease; if knowledge, it will be brought to nothing.
[9]For we know partially and we prophesy partially,
[10]but when the perfect comes, the partial will pass
away. [11]When I was a child, I used to talk as a child,
think as a child, reason as a child; when I became
a man, I put aside childish things. [12]At present we
see indistinctly, as in a mirror, but then face to face.
At present I know partially; then I shall know fully,
as I am fully known. [13]So faith, hope, love remain,
these three; but the greatest of these is love.

Paul writes these words because he believes that if the spiritual gifts are used in love, they will build up his fractured Corinthian community. But 1 Corinthians 13:1-13 transcends its context. It identifies the grounding of the divine-human relationship in which every Christian believer stands.

The passage easily divides into three sections: verses 1-3, 4-7, and 8-13. The first section forcibly asserts that no action or gift has value without love. Speaking in tongues, prophesying, even handing over one's body as a sacrifice amount to "nothing" without love (vv. 2, 3). Again, love here is more than an emotion. It is our very life with God. Doing anything without being grounded in that relationship is of no benefit.

The second section (vv. 4-7) lists fifteen qualities of love. Some of these qualities gravitate more toward our way of loving, while other qualities incline more toward God's way

Paul and the Corinthians

The situation Paul addresses in his First Letter to the Corinthians is disunity within the community. Some Corinthians claimed that their superior wisdom made them better than others (1:10—4:21). Others used pagan law courts to resolve disputes that should have been settled among themselves (6:1-11). Still others insisted that their spiritual gifts were the most important (12:1-31; 14:1-40). Even the celebration of the Eucharist was marred by social differences (11:17-22).

Paul believes that love can unite the Corinthians. He calls them to practice it ("Your every act should be done with love," 16:14; also 8:1) and includes the great hymn to love in chapter 13 to extol it. It is ironic that this greatest exposition of love in the New Testament was occasioned by pride and bickering within one of the earliest Christian communities.

of loving. Still others apply to both. Patience and kindness (v. 4), for example, can certainly refer to our love, but they are also regularly used to express God's love (e.g., Rom 2:4). "Kind[ness]" here may well express God's "loving-kindness," or *hesed*. In verse 6, "truth" should be understood in the biblical sense of "fidelity"—God's fidelity to us and our fidelity to God. Several qualities of love in verses 4-7 are presented without assigning them either to God or us. The ambivalent mix seems intentional. Love is the characteristic that applies to both sides of the divine-human relationship. It is in love that our covenant with God is lived.

Verse 7 anticipates the final verse in the passage (v. 13). It connects faith and hope to love. Love "*believes* all things" and "*hopes* all things" (emphasis added). Here Paul tells us that love is what makes faith and hope possible. Faith and hope can only exist when they are energized by the interchange of love between God and us.

In the third section of the passage (vv. 8-13), Paul turns toward the future. He knows that faith is believing God has initiated the kingdom in the death and resurrection of Jesus and that hope is trusting in Christ's return to fully establish that kingdom. He now assures us that love will carry us to that ultimate victory: "Love never fails" (v. 8). All the spiritual gifts will cease. But love is forever. The spiritual gifts are partial ways in which God interacts with us. When Christ returns, when the kingdom comes, such gifts will not be necessary (v. 10). Paul then uses two images to illustrate this movement from partial to perfect. It is like maturing from a child to an adult (v. 11). It is like seeing face-to-face rather than catching a reflection in a mirror (v. 12). This second image alludes to a personal relationship, for the face we will see is the face of God.

Paul concludes by returning to the three dynamics that define our relationship with God: faith, hope, and love. He asserts that love is the greatest, the most important (v. 13). Here we arrive at the concluding insight of our study. Why does Paul elevate love to the highest place in the holy triad? Because love is the very life we share with God. If faith is entering and clinging to the relationship, if hope is trusting that the promises of the relationship will be fulfilled, love is the relationship itself.

Conclusion

Fully comprehending the mystery of our covenant relationship with God is impossible. As Paul says, now we see "indistinctly, as in a mirror" (1 Cor 13:12). But what we can see is guided by faith, hope, and love. Through them we enter into and cling to a relationship that we believe God has freely initiated, and in them we trust that the promises God has made to us are real and worthy of our hope. But faith, hope, and love also show us that if we want to know why God began this relationship, what God expects of us in it, and how we are to treat our neighbor because of it, the best answer is love.

When the kingdom comes and we see God face-to-face, faith will no longer be necessary. For then we will behold the One in whom we have believed. When God's new creation is fully established at Christ's return, hope will disappear. For then we will possess all that can be hoped for. But on that great last day, love will remain. Love must remain. For love is the giving and receiving that constitutes our life with God. Love is the relationship that began with Abraham, reaches its height in Jesus, and transfers our love for God even to our enemy. Love is the covenant that has joined us to God forever.

"So faith, hope, love remain, these three; but the greatest of these is love" (1 Cor 13:13).

EXPLORING LESSON SIX

1. How do you worship? How is your worship an expression of your love for God?

2. Scripture emphasizes the importance of loving God with one's whole self (e.g., Deut 6:5). How would you explain in your own words, based on your own experience, what it means to love God with your whole heart, your whole being, and your whole strength?

3. a) What does the commentary mean by the expression *transferred love*?

   b) Have you always considered your love for others to be an expression of your love for God? Or is this a new (or newly refreshed) connection for you? Can you think of particular examples of *transferred love* in your own life?

4. What is the Great Commandment of Jesus (Matt 22:37-40; Mark 12:29-34; Luke 10:25-28)?

5. How does the parable of the Good Samaritan offer further instruction from Jesus on what it means to love our neighbor (Luke 10:29-37)?

6. a) What about Jesus' command to love our enemies (Matt 5:44) is consistent with the Hebrew Scriptures? What is new about this command?

   b) Reflect on a time when you have been able to love an enemy. As you look back on this experience, how do you see it as a time of grace and an expression of your love for God?

7. What is the Gospel of John's version of *transferred love* (John 10:30; 13:34; 14:21)?

8. How is Jesus' command to love one another in John's Gospel a *new* command (John 13:34)? How has Jesus "raised the bar" on love with this command (John 15:13)?

9. What are the fifteen qualities of love listed in 1 Corinthians 13:4-7? Which one of these qualities do you find the most challenging to live? Which one comes most naturally to you?

10. What insight about our love for God can you share with your group after studying and reflecting on the Scripture texts explored in this lesson?

CLOSING PRAYER

We love because he first loved us. (1 John 4:19)

God of love, you loved and chose us in Christ before the foundation of the world (Eph 1:4). May we respond by loving you with all our hearts, minds, and strength, and by loving others as you love us. We give you thanks for the time we have spent together studying your word. We pray now in gratitude for one another, especially . . .

PRAYING WITH YOUR GROUP

Because we know that the Bible allows us to hear God's voice, prayer provides the context for our study and sharing. By speaking and listening to God and each other, the discussion often grows to more deeply bond us to one another and to God.

At *the beginning and end of each lesson* simple prayers are provided for individual use, and also may be used within the group setting. Most of the closing prayers provided with each lesson relate directly to a theme from that lesson and encourage you to pray together for people and events in your local community.

Of course, there are many ways to center ourselves in God's presence as we gather together in groups around the word of God. We provide some additional suggestions here knowing you and your group will make prayer a priority as part of your gathering. These are simply alternative ways to pray if your group would like to try something different from those prayers provided in the previous pages.

Conversational Prayer

This form of prayer allows for the group members to pray in their own words in a way that is not intimidating. The group leader begins with Step One, inviting all to focus on the presence of Christ among them. After a few moments of quiet, the group leader invites anyone in the group to voice a prayer or two of thanksgiving; once that is complete, then anyone who has personal intentions may pray in their own words for their needs; finally, the group prays for the needs of others.

A suggested process:
In your own words, speak simple and short prayers to allow time for others to add their voices.

Focus on one "step" at a time, not worrying about praying for everything in your mental list at once.

Step One	Visualize Christ. Welcome him. Imagine him present with you in your group. Allow time for some silence.
Step Two	Gratitude opens our hearts. Use simple words such as, "Thank you, Lord, for . . ."
Step Three	Pray for your own needs knowing that others will pray with you. Be specific and honest. Use "I" and "me" language.

Step Four	Pray for others by name, with love. You may voice your agreement ("Yes, Lord"). End with gratitude for sharing concerns.

Praying Like Ignatius

St. Ignatius Loyola, whose life and ministry are the foundation of the Jesuit community, invites us to enter into Scripture texts in order to experience the scenes, especially scenes of the gospels or other narrative parts of Scripture. Simply put, this is a method of creatively imagining the scene, viewing it from the inside, and asking God to meet you there. Most often, this is a personal form of prayer, but in a group setting, some of its elements can be helpful if you allow time for this process.

A suggested process:

- Select a scene from the chapters in the particular lesson.
- Read that scene out loud in the group, followed by some quiet time.
- Ask group members to place themselves in the scene (as a character, or as an onlooker) so that they can imagine the emotions, responses, and thinking that may have taken place. Notice the details and the tone, and imagine the interaction with the Lord that is taking place.
- Share with the group any insights that came to you in this quiet imagining.
- Allow each person in the group to thank God for some insight and to pray about some request that may have surfaced.

Sacred Reading (or Lectio Divina)

This method of prayer invites us to "listen with the ear of the heart" as St. Benedict's rule would say. We listen to the words and the phrasing, asking God to speak to our innermost being. Again, this method of prayer is most often used in an individual setting but may also be used in an adapted way within a group.

A suggested process:

- Select a scene from the chapters in the particular lesson.
- Read the scene out loud in the group, perhaps two times.
- Ask group members to ponder a word or phrase that stands out to them.
- The group members could then simply speak the word or phrase as a kind of litany of what was meaningful for your group.
- Allow time for more silence to ponder the words that were heard, asking God to reveal to you what message you are meant to hear, how God is speaking to you.
- Follow up with spoken intentions at the close of this group time.

REFLECTING ON SCRIPTURE

Reading Scripture is an opportunity not simply to learn new information but to listen to God who loves you. Pray that the same Holy Spirit who guided the formation of Scripture will inspire you to correctly understand what you read, and empower you to make what you read a part of your life.

The inspired word of God contains layers of meaning. As you make your way through passages of Scripture, whether studying a book of the Bible or focusing on a biblical theme, you may find it helpful to ask yourself these four questions:

What does the Scripture passage say?
Read the passage slowly and reflectively. Become familiar with it. If the passage you are reading is a narrative, carefully observe the characters and the plot. Use your imagination to picture the scene or enter into it.

What does the Scripture passage mean?
Read the footnotes in your Bible and the commentary provided to help you understand what the sacred writers intended and what God wants to communicate by means of their words.

What does the Scripture passage mean to me?
Meditate on the passage. God's word is living and powerful. What is God saying to you? How does the Scripture passage apply to your life today?

What am I going to do about it?
Try to discover how God may be challenging you in this passage. An encounter with God contains a challenge to know God's will and follow it more closely in daily life. Ask the Holy Spirit to inspire not only your mind but your life with this living word.